Thoughts

The Power of Your Mind

Peter Allman, MA

For all Writer's Groups

Table of Contents

Introduction

Companion Guide (Cheat Sheet)

Thoughts

The power of your mind

Everything starts with a thought. Putting fluoride in water, a school-yard fight, being kind to your spouse when you'd rather yell. Hitler exterminating Jews – all these things started with a thought. Evidence of thoughts is everywhere. Thoughts come from our mind. The mind is a wonderful servant but a terrible master. This book will help you train your mind to become the "wonderful servant" you need to lead a happy and healthy life.

How can the mind be a terrible master? What were you thinking a minute ago? According to the National Science Foundation, that thought is one of about 50 that you have every minute, every waking minute of every day. That's up to 50,000 thoughts per day! If your mind is constantly scampering around like a squirrel on caffeine (or crack cocaine), how can you find peace and serenity?

The number of thoughts we have each day is staggering, but even more staggering is the idea that we tend to repeat thoughts from our past. If those thoughts are negative, unproductive, and unhealthy, our days will be full of suffering. Our minds will be a terrible master.

Can you imagine being able to shape, control, and access the power of your minute to minute thinking? Living with a mind that is quiet and composed? Sounds like a slice of heaven.

This book uses the wisdom of thought leaders through the ages. Each chapter contains a provocative quote from a philosopher, artist, author, spiritual leader, scientist, statesman, or theologian to help you train your mind to be a wonderful servant. The twenty-six chapters literally cover the wisdom from A to Z: from Aristotle, who lived from 384 to 322 BC, to the thinking of modern-day spiritual writer Gary Zukav. This wisdom will show you that there is nothing new under the sun—all are saying the same thing—your thoughts create your reality.

Together, we're going to explore the power of your thoughts. You will "see" your thoughts and that will create room to work with those thoughts. You will have the flexibility to decide whether to act on that thought or discard it and create a healthier one.

To expand your awareness of your thinking, and to help you understand how your life is dominated by your thoughts, here is a list of words that are aspects of a thought:

view	expectation	paradigm	theory
idea	answer	notion	inspiration
image	concept	opinion	brainstorm
script	intention	interpretation	consideration
ideal	deliberation	reflection	musing
belief	attitude	perspective	question
dream	judgment	outlook	attitude
story	question		

Can you see how thinking dominates your life? By reading this book, you've already taken the first step to better understand how thinking affects you, use better mental strategies, and create a happier and healthier life.

Keep reading and let's explore how to put your mind to work for you.

Life Changing Truths

Here are three life-changing truths that have been talked about for centuries.

Truth #1: Your thoughts create your reality. What is real to you is a world of your own creation. You may take your mental processing and production to be reality, but it is not. Your experience of life is your thoughts creating the illusion of reality. This may be difficult to understand, but what it means is that if you are in a good mood, content, or peaceful, you have created that with your thoughts. How? By not fighting external conditions—"what is." You accept the situation and have non-judgmental thoughts. This is not a laissez-faire or defeatist attitude. In fact, it is a powerful way to *be* in the world. It is an attitude that gives you freedom to operate in a healthy, flexible, and peaceful way. If you are not in a good mood, it means that your thinking is judgmental, and does not accept what is happening in the outside world.

Most people would argue they are not free from their conditions. They complain about the conditions of their work, the habits of their spouse, the lack of appreciation from their children, the stupidity of the political system, and so on.

These conditions do not lead inevitably to suffering. It is your perspective on each condition that leads to suffering or peace. An unpleasant situation is "real" in the way that you experience it. What if your first step is to accept it? You will then have the mental space and freedom to create more functional thoughts, maneuver and communicate effectively to your spouse, your boss, your children, and your elected political official. State what you need. State how their behavior affects you. Compromise. Practice these healthy coping strategies with an open mind and heart and without being attached to the other person's behaviors. You may then be able to create a more peaceful situation.

The way you operate in your internal and external worlds always starts in the internal world of thoughts. Your thoughts then create your feelings. The information from your thoughts and feelings leads you to choose your behaviors.

Thought

Feelings

Behavior

Truth #2: There is no reality outside your interpretation of it. There are objective realities like a car or a prime rib dinner, but these are open to a variety of interpretations. For example, the car might be a Chevrolet. One person might say, "I'm a fourth generation Chevy owner. They are the best cars!" Another person might say, "Chevys are a piece of junk! I'm a Ford guy." Or, "I'm on a protein diet and lost 20 pounds. I'm ordering prime rib for lunch." Another person might say, "I'm a vegetarian. Eating meat is a disservice to our environment and the animals. I would never order prime rib." Their thoughts create their reality.

The world does not automatically make sense to us. We create our own ways of understanding our world. An event is merely a piece of information. Because it gives rise to thoughts or interpretations, it can create many feelings and behaviors. Each person can view the world only through the lenses of his or her own choosing.

Let's look at an event that proves this point. Susie's friends are throwing a party. Susie has invited her friend

Terri by calling and texting. Terri has not responded to either communication:

1) Susie *thinks* it's because Terri doesn't care about the friendship anymore.
2) Susie's friend Dee *thinks* it's because Terri is super busy at work.
3) Susie's mom *thinks* it's because Terri has Attention Deficit Disorder and has simply gotten lost in her own world and forgot to respond.
4) Another friend, Abby, *thinks* Terri doesn't know the etiquette of responding and will probably just show up.

So who's right? They are all right—in their own minds. Since everything starts with a thought, they will all experience their own personal emotional and relational consequences from their thoughts.

The same darned event, yet it has four different interpretations. Four different people with four different thoughts, who construed the meaning of the same event in four different ways. How did each of these thoughts affect that specific person?

1) Susie got angry, pouted, and had a miserable couple of days.
2) Dee didn't think any more about it and had good days.
3) Susie's mom felt a little bad for Susie and Terri, but didn't let it affect her days.
4) Abby was hopeful she would run into Terri, but also let it go and didn't lose her peace.

At our core, we want peace and happiness in our lives. To achieve this for myself, I work on not resisting life and creating more productive thoughts about the conditions in my world. Epictetus, a Greek Stoic philosopher, and Marcus Aurelius, a Roman Emperor, said more than two millennia ago that it's not our experiences that form us but the ways in which we respond to them.

Truth #3 You are not your thoughts. Thoughts are merely thoughts. They are illusory. You cannot touch a thought. It may feel heavy and "real," but you can change a thought and feel better as a result. Through the practice of meditation, you can "see" your thoughts and the associated feelings, and then through this space of awareness, determine which thoughts are healthy and which unhealthy.. Choosing a healthier thought can help you respond to the world in a compassionate way, rather than reacting in a hostile way.

Psychiatrist and Holocaust survivor Viktor Frankl said, "Between stimulus and response there is a space. In that space is our power to choose our response. In our response lies our growth and our freedom." When a stimulus occurs; for example, your significant other doesn't follow through, or your children are acting out, there is a space before you respond where you can "see" your thoughts. For example, you have asked your children twice to get ready for bed. The stimulus is that the children are still glued to the TV. In the space, you "see" many thoughts rumbling through your brain. Here are three possible thoughts. (1) *I'm going to yell at them. (2) Relax, turn the TV off and speak firmly about doing bedtime routines. (3) It's time to get my spouse to step in.* You can respond with the most functional and productive thought.

You can be aware of the thoughts that lead you to lash out or say angry words. Growth and freedom occur when you don't attach to those reactive thoughts, but rather create different thoughts that allow you to respond in a healthier way (and you won't have to circle back and ask for forgiveness).

Thoughts themselves are not the problem. It is the nature of your mind to create thoughts. Attaching and identifying to negative thoughts and acting in an unhealthy way are the problem. Picture yourself in a garden. You see flowers, vegetables, and weeds in the garden. You are watering the garden by hand. Naturally, you choose to water the flowers and vegetables because you want them to grow. You choose to not water the weeds, because you do not want them to grow. It's the same with thoughts. You can create positive mental states by "watering" those thoughts and then manifesting healthy behaviors— flowers—in the world. You can choose to not "water" the negative, unproductive thoughts. You will then create more heavenly and fewer hellish experiences here on earth.

In the western world, these three truths are not typically taught and stressed in parenting classes, school, or weekly meetings at work. In each chapter, I include a client's story to analyze how these three truths play out in real life. This process of repetition is a good way to integrate new ways of thinking. It will be then easier to practice living these ways in your daily life.

Re-write Your Own Story

"It weighs on my mind," is a common statement of someone who is stuck on some specific life event. He or she has a thought that is running over and over, like a looping video. He or she is suffering. Some thoughts are heavy and depressing. In the Broadway play *Wicked,* the character Elphaba is tired of being viewed as the wicked witch and not finding love. In the song *Defying Gravity,* she says,

"I'm through accepting limits," (that is a thought),

"Some things I cannot change," (another thought),

"But till I try, I'll never know," (another thought),

15

"I'm defying gravity and you can't pull me down."

(another thought).

This is a concrete example of healthy thoughts that helped Elphaba escape something that was weighing on her mind—a depressing situation—and got her on the road to freedom and joy. When you watch a movie or a television show, you can sometimes believe that what you are watching is truth. You believe the pixels on the screen are real. Your muscles tense when there is a stressful situation. You might cry when the potential lover leaves the girl behind.

Your internal world of thoughts creates the "movie" that is playing in front of you—in your external world. Your muscles might get tense when a conflict occurs and you *think* it's bad and terrible. You might become sad when you *think* your child is not playing well in an athletic event or school play.

For a while, your mind does not know the difference between the movie on the screen and your life. Truth #1 states "Your thoughts create your reality." You have thoughts that tell you that what is happening in the movie theater is real—just like your life when you walk out of the theater and back to your car. Truth #2 states "There is no reality outside your interpretation of it." You interpret the pixels as real just as after the movie you deem that the guy in the lobby is a jerk because he didn't open the door for his girlfriend. Truth #3 states "You are not your thoughts." The thoughts that the pixels are "real" is not who you are. You merely suspended belief while you were in the theater.

The light in the movie projector projects the images up on the big screen. Your awareness of your thoughts is like the light in the projector. Awareness or consciousness allows you to "see" that if you act on a certain thought, your movie might have a negative ending. With awareness, you can change the thought, which will then create a new behavior and project a different "movie" with a better ending.

Sounds simple, but simple is not always easy. The truths from this book will help you create a healthier, happier, and more productive life. That might sound like a big promise. But your thoughts create your reality. If you really want a better reality—a better life—you can practice being aware of your thoughts, change the thoughts when necessary, and create the behavior(s) and outcome(s) that you want. You mind will be a wonderful servant.

Remember that thoughts are not you. Change your thoughts so your life—the "movie"—has better outcomes and happier endings. For example, create the thought that conflicts can be beneficial and talking about them can bring you and your spouse or friend closer together. Create the thought of spending time with your child and asking open-ended questions to help him or her process lingering issues. Remember that a situation is open to a variety of interpretations. You might be disappointed because your child didn't play well in a basketball game, but your child might not feel the same way about his athletic performance. You might even find out that your child would rather play a musical instrument than be on the basketball team.

How do you like those two new movies? Do they make you feel better? They are lighter, healthier, and more productive because you created distance between your initial thoughts of fear and judgment, changed those thoughts, and created more productive and healthier outcomes -- a better movie.

Let's Start Re-writing It Now

Radical comes from the Latin word "radix," meaning root. For something to be radical it has to cut to the core of the issue and deal with root causes, not just symptoms. This book is radical because it challenges you to look at your thoughts, which are the roots. The symptoms are the "movies" that are playing out in front of you.

You know about cause and effect. Let's flip this concept: your life and your feelings are the *effect* of an earlier *cause*. The "causes" are your thoughts which lead to your actions. The "effects" are the conditions of your life. If you don't like the effect, change the cause—your thoughts! This book will help you get at the root—your thoughts— which will inevitably affect your life.

Fads come and go. Truth lasts and perseveres through the ages. This book contains truth from more than 26 renowned philosophers, authors, scientists, and theologians from 500 B.C. to the 21st century. This book contains truth from many religions and schools of thought. If a Buddhist thought matches a Native American thought which matches a Christian thought, it must be truth.

I am a psychotherapist who has been helping people for 25 years. I will share some clinical examples and clients' therapeutic insights in this book. I think this is helpful, but what could be even more helpful is the idea that **A**ristotle, **B**uddha, **C**hurchill, and all the sages to the end of the alphabet, are basically saying the same thing.

Each of the twenty-six chapters stands alone. The thought (quote) for each chapter reflects how your life can be happier and more productive. There are three "Reflections" at the end of each chapter which will help you practice living a new, healthier way of living. The book is written and structured in a way that includes some repetition. The idea of creating "healthier and more productive thoughts" is repeated frequently. That is done intentionally, with the goal of helping you create the habit of not judging things as "good" or "bad" but as healthy or unhealthy, productive or not productive for you as you create a new way of thinking and being.

The yellow brick road starts here. In The Wizard of Oz Dorothy did not walk directly to the Emerald City. She took a circuitous route with many obstacles. You will too. That's okay. . With a better understanding of how your mind works, practice and practice some more. You will find a true wizard—not a fake behind a curtain. *You* are the "wizard." *You* are your own guru, spiritual leader, and sage. *You* will find your way back home.

Chapter 1

A

"It is the mark of an educated mind to be able to entertain a thought without accepting it."

Aristotle

Aristotle lived from 384 to 322 BC. He was a Greek philosopher who, along with Plato, is considered the father of western philosophy. He tutored Alexander the Great. His teachings influenced Islamic thought as well as Christian theology.

Your mind works like a computer. Your mind has "files" where it stores information on everything in your life. Two of your biggest files are about yourself and the people with whom you spend the most time. In a computer, a corrupt file wreaks havoc. If you were taught negative things about yourself, it's as if you have a corrupted file in your mind. You might have been told you are not smart. You then have thoughts in your mind about your limited ability in school. You might have been told you are too skinny or too fat and may have a corrupted file in your mind about your body.

A computer's search engine is fueled by data. When you are interacting in the world, your mind is fueled by data and the result is the thoughts you have learned and accepted as truth. So, for example, if you learned something negative about yourself in the past, your mind, in the present moment, is taking in information and running through that data. Your mind creates thoughts after the search is complete. "He won't like me because I'm too fat." "I won't do well in school because I'm not that smart."

By going to counseling, reading this and other self-help books, and attending support groups, you become more *educated* and aware that you are not your thoughts. You can learn that the unhealthy, toxic information you learned during childhood is a lie. You can then practice "seeing" those thoughts but not accepting them.

Mary was a client who grew up in an emotionally abusive home. Her single mother was resentful that the child's father didn't stay around, and her world had been turned upside down by having a child. She took out her negativity on Mary throughout her childhood. The child received many harmful messages while growing up. One of the messages the mom told her was that she was manipulative and she used people. Mary learned that and had those thoughts running through her mind as a child, adolescent, and adult. She didn't like those thoughts, so she always tried to do the opposite. She helped everyone she could. As an adult, she lent money to people knowing she probably wouldn't get paid back. She gave and gave and gave which always turned out to be at her expense. All her relationships were win-lose. She became co-dependent, and her well-being was always based on how others were doing in life.

Let's see how Mary's case fits into the three truths:

Truth #1: *Your thoughts create your reality.* Mary's reality—her self-concept—was negatively programmed by her mother. Mary's reality is a corrupt file that says "You are manipulative." "You use people." On the other hand, people who interacted with Mary would share their reality with her: "You are so kind." "You are one of the nicest people I know." "I've met no one as thoughtful as you." These two realities are 180 degrees apart.

Truth #2: *There is no reality outside your interpretation of it.* Other people's realities, their thoughts of Mary, did not fit with the reality in her mind. She would discount her friends' interpretations and continue to be driven by the thoughts she learned in childhood. This kind of thinking creates a vicious circle . One can exit this circle through awareness, and replacing the old, non-productive thoughts with better ones.

Truth #3: *You are not your thoughts.* The work Mary did in therapy was to realize she did what any other child would have done—believe what a parent told her. Mary came to understand that her mom was miserable and took it out on Mary. She came to understand that her mom felt manipulated and used by Mary's father and projected those thoughts on Mary. Mary then understood she was not those toxic words her mother reflected to her. They were merely her mother's thoughts and they were merely thoughts she had accepted and integrated. She realized she could create new thoughts which would make her feel better about herself, and then make healthier decisions. Mary would still have the thoughts of "I am not a user of people and to prove that I will give, give, and give some more." With awareness, she "entertained" that thought, but did not accept it, let go of it, and created new thoughts. The new thought, "I want to take care of myself along with taking care of others," is a healthy, balanced thought that creates win-win outcomes.

If our thinking is too one-sided, we tend to correct by overcompensating. Mary did that by being a martyr, which simply created another corrupt file. That overcorrection did not create peace and happiness.

Thoughts that create balance—the middle way—are the healthiest and most productive. It is important to have thoughts that move you to take care of others. It is equally important to have thoughts that move you to take care of self.

Mary's mom is still alive and they communicate sporadically. Mary's mom still communicates toxic messages to Mary. Her mom is like a computer virus which is a malicious software that changes other computer programs and inserts its own code. Firewalls stop computer viruses. For humans, healthy boundaries stop other people's negative messages. Mary learned to not accept her mother's messages and limit their conversations. She also practiced a powerful strategy by speaking her new thoughts about how she will live in the world out loud in front of a mirror.

Every day, every moment, we need to be aware of our thoughts, and mentally create a little distance from them. A Buddhist strategy is to picture your thoughts as clouds; they are temporary formations and they slowly dissipate. Meditation teachers have suggested imagining thoughts as if they are on a river and then watching them naturally flow away. Any practice that creates mental distance from your thoughts, and helps you realize thoughts are ethereal, will give you the space and freedom to *entertain* the thoughts and decide if you are going to accept them or let go of them and replace them with healthier thoughts.

For me, driving a car is when my thinking can go sideways. My mind wanders to what a friend said to me, what a family member did or did not do, work-related issues, or all the demands on me. The list can go on and on.

Before I was aware of the practice of meditation and mindfulness, I would unconsciously hang on to those toxic thoughts—the corrupted files—and either stuff them and experience anger and anxiety, or take them out on other people.

I read about people's comments at the end of their lives. They are now in a mental state where they see their thoughts and life more clearly. The share that they wished they would have made different decisions and not gone with the cultural and family norms. In other words, they wished they had entertained different thoughts. Jack Kerouac, the leader of the 1960's Beat movement, wrote about his travels with a friend across America in *On the Road*. They ran into a farmer in Nebraska, and he said, "You guys are going somewhere or just going?" Be aware of your thoughts so you drive your life to the "somewhere" you want to go.

Author Michael Singer wrote, "There is nothing more important to true growth than realizing you are not the voice of the mind—you are the one who hears it." Thich Nhat Hanh, the Vietnamese Buddhist monk, peace activist, and author of more than seventy books said, "Meditation is to be aware of what is going on: in your body, in your feelings, in your mind, in the world." These are the files that run the computer. For a variety of reasons, we all have corrupted files—dysfunctional thoughts. Since everything begins with a thought, we must be aware of them. We can then change the thoughts and create healthier thoughts, which will lead us to a happier life.

Reflections
1. Name a "corrupt file" that is keeping you stuck in life.
2. Replace that unhealthy thought with a more productive thought.

3. How does that feel? What were the changes in your life?

Chapter 2

B

"You are what you think. Pain will follow bad thoughts as certain as happiness will follow good ones."

Buddha

Siddhartha, who later became known as the Buddha, or The Enlightened One, was a prince who left the comforts of his palace to seek a way to eliminate suffering in the world. He was born in India around 400 BC.

In the introduction, I described how humans operate. Everything starts with a thought, which creates a feeling, which then leads us to take a certain action. In the quote above, Buddha is saying that a thought will create a feeling of either pain or happiness. Pretty simple. If I interviewed 100 people, 100 of them would say they would rather have happiness than pain in their lives. So why do so many of us experience more pain than happiness? Obviously, simple is not easy.

Understanding where thoughts come from is the first step in answering this question. I believe there are two main sources of our thoughts: from the "ego mind" and from the mind that is connected to God/Higher Self/True Self/Spirit, or any language that tries to explain that which is greater than we are

The ego mind always leads to destruction, pain, and suffering. The ego mind tricks us and promises it will be our friend, take care of us, and make us better than others, but it is like a parasite: it will harm and ultimately destroy us.

Our ego mind can only exist in the past or the future. It tricks us into staying connected with it by judging others, staying busy, and looking for successes and affirmations in the external world. It gains power when we view ourselves as separate from others and then create win-lose outcomes. The ego mind is empowered when we only identify with our problems, our things- to-do lists, and our narrow view of the world.

The ego mind wants to attack those who disagree with us or who look different than us. The ego also attacks us. The ego sets up a high bar—one that is really not achievable. Then, when we don't meet the goals, it creates thoughts that say we're not good enough, bad, and wrong. Pain ensues.

Living from the ego mind leads us to think that we're in charge, and we can will anything into existence. These descriptions and thought processes are void of the Source which is greater than us. One could say that the three letters of ego could stand for edging God out.

When I have operated from the ego mind, it is only a matter of time before I experience pain. Sometimes my first reaction is to blame others—which is another trick of the ego mind. The journey toward happiness is always first inward; watching and monitoring my unhealthy thoughts. I quiet my mind and get connected to my Source. Then, with this awareness, I can change them to thoughts that allows happiness to follow.

We can change our mode of thinking by seeing how we are being used by the ego mind. We can let go of the thoughts that create pain and practice identifying with and acting with our Higher Self.

Solomon is the Biblical king most famous for his wisdom. He said in Proverbs 4:7, "With all thy getting, get understanding." All the great spiritual teachers have said that we need to de-power our ego mind, and empower our mind that is connected to Spirit. Understanding and practicing this will lead to happiness and "heaven on earth." That is freedom.

Thoughts move like boomerangs and will ultimately bring back to us exactly what we send out. Jesus said, "As you sow, so shall ye reap." The Buddhists and Hindus believe in the law of karma, which states that one's volitional action, whether of word, thought, or deed, has a consequence that returns to that person, i.e., "what goes around comes around." All these examples are saying the same thing: *pain will follow unhealthy thoughts as certain as happiness will follow healthy ones.*

We learned many of the ways we think and process life in childhood. Sadly, one of the concepts many of us learn by the end of elementary school is that the Universe is essentially hostile to human interests. We are taught the main way to "survive" is to be competitive or lose at life. We don't want to be on the losing side, so we fight hard to win. This creates win-lose outcomes which further perpetuates this painful way to live in the world. Ironically, ego will not let winners win because it's never enough.

There are government initiatives that continue this line of battle field thinking. The "war on drugs" and the "war on poverty" are examples of this mentality. Wars do not create healthy and life-sustaining outcomes. Wars create pain, harm, losers, fear, and hostility toward the winners. Individual egos and the corporate cultural ego are in charge with this mentality. And, have we won the war on drugs or poverty?

The opposite of this view—or another way to *think*—is to be cooperative, work together, and create win-win outcomes. Cooperation creates mutual happiness, prosperity, love, and long- term successes. The Spirit is in charge at an individual and collective level.

Each of these ways of thinking creates a self-fulfilling prophecy. If one sees life as hostile, that person will try to create battles with others so he or she will "win." Thinking that the structure of reality is hostile will create the groundwork for battles.

The opposite is also a self-fulfilling prophecy. If the Universe is friendly, it is natural to think and work in a more communal, consensual way. Both sides get what they need and happiness ensues. If we see the structure of the Universe as working toward goodness, we will create scenarios where positive outcomes are a natural and realistic goal.

Let's see how these types of thinking fit into the three truths in the Introduction:

Truth #1: *Your thoughts create your reality.* The world is competitive, because we make it that way. It's like the goldfish in a bowl that only has 12 inches in which to swim. If that goldfish is put into a bathtub, the goldfish continues to swim in a 12 inch circle. The structure of reality is not innately competitive. There are models of working in harmony, collaboration, and community. But if we are not exposed to these types of thinking, we will be like the goldfish continuing to swim in the size of his old bowl. We will be oblivious to larger ways of "swimming" in the world.

Truth #2: *There is no reality outside your interpretation.* Men are from Mars and women are from Venus. Although there are plenty of exceptions, men generally see life—through thought patterns—as hierarchical, competitive, and naturally take care of themselves. With the same exceptions, women see life—through thought patterns—as relational, cyclical, and naturally take care of others. Both are real to each gender. Each interprets life differently. Another form of reality is a combination of the two, which the Chinese refer to as the "yin-yang." This reality takes care of self and takes care of others and it can create win-win outcomes.

Truth #3: *You are not your thoughts.* A woman is in counseling because she has been an unhealthy martyr. She gives, gives, and gives to others while ignoring her own needs. During counseling, she learned a new way of thinking. She learned to incorporate the masculine traits of setting boundaries, saying no, and setting aside time for herself. This woman was never actually a martyr, because if she had been, that reality would never change. Her old thinking made her a martyr. Her new thinking has created a healthier way for her to live in the world.

Edmund Hillary, the first climber to reach the summit of Mount Everest said, "It is not the mountain we conquer, but ourselves." Do not look to the external world to change or conquer. Look within, see your habitual way of thinking, and change from the ego mind to the mind of your higher self. Then you can more peacefully and efficiently scale any "mountain" in front of you.

Reflections
1. Where is there pain in your life? Find the associated thought that is creating that pain.
2. Find a more healthy and functional thought that will create more happiness in your life.
3. Become more conscious of your thoughts. See when your ego mind is in charge. Spend time letting go of that thought, and create a thought from your spiritual source. How does that feel?

Chapter 3

C

"The pessimist sees difficulty in every opportunity. The optimist sees opportunity in every difficulty."

Winston Churchill

Winston Churchill was Prime Minister of the United Kingdom from 1940-1945, and again from 1951-1955. Churchill's charismatic leadership and strong communication skills helped Great Britain defeat the Nazis in World War II. In 1953, Churchill was awarded the Nobel Prize in Literature "for his mastery of historical and biographical description as well as for brilliant oratory in defending human values."

In the Introduction, I used a metaphor to illuminate how thoughts create our reality. I said that when you watch a movie, you suspend the belief that you are in a movie theater and only watching projected lights and shadows on a screen. You believe what you see in front of you. You cry, become tense, and laugh.

In your life, you create a "movie" that is playing in front of you. Your thoughts interpret, judge, and create a story about your life circumstances. This happens easily because we are story-telling creatures. We make sense of the world by the stories we tell ourselves about it.

Stories are a series of thoughts that are tied together. For example, a 50-year-old man, dressed in a suit, is in front of you at the coffee shop. In that moment, you could have a variety of thoughts. Do you realize that you can decide which thought to embrace? For example, you could think, "Another rich guy, buying $8.00 drinks, only thinking of himself. He should donate the $40 a week to a homeless shelter." You feel agitated and unhappy that he is in the same coffee shop as you. Not a very good movie.

Or, you could be neutral with your thoughts about him. "There are only two people ahead of me. That's pretty good for a Monday morning." Your thoughts wander. "I have to remember to talk to Gail when I get to work about the Perry project." This movie does not have highs or lows.

A third way to think about it is with thoughts that create a storyline filled with empathy and love. "This businessman is dressed well, but he looks tired and the weight of the world is on his shoulders. His job is probably very stressful. I will send him a quick healing prayer and create a situation where I can share a smile with him." This movie has meaning and it always feels good to do good.

The beauty of being human is that the choice is yours. *The Little Engine That Could* is a wonderful book published in 1930. The story tells of a long train that must be pulled over a high mountain because its engine has broken and cannot be repaired. A variety of big and strong engines refused to pull that stranded train. Finally, a small engine agrees to try and pull the train over the mountain. This engine succeeds by repeating a certain thought to itself, "I think I can. I think I can." The Little Engine felt good about itself and brought great benefit to the people on the other side of the mountain.

This story turns out well because of optimistic thoughts. A pessimist—the other engines—perceived too much difficulty and did not risk trying to pull the train. In this fairytale, the optimistic little engine created a good story, a good "movie," a good life for itself. The pessimist stayed stuck, did not have good stories to tell its children, and became even more bored and unhappy. He will forever wonder what else he might have accomplished.

How does a person become more optimistic or pessimistic? You are the writer, director, producer, and lead actor in your movie—your life. If you were handed a script from your parents that saw the world pessimistically, throw it out and write a better script! If you want to blame your parents for your life script, you will remain a pessimist.

Our thoughts—our script—are programmed early. We learn how to perceive the world through the lens of our parents, grandparents, older siblings, cultural group, and other people close to us. If you learn from these people that you cannot trust the world, that people are out to get you, and rarely are there safe places in the world, your mind will be programmed to think pessimistically. The opposite is also true. If your caregivers teach you that most people are trustworthy, you can use your discerning mind and know there are many safe environments where you can share yourself and grow, and you will think more optimistically.

Henry Ford, the founder of Ford Motor Company, said, "Whether you think you can or whether you think you can't, you're right." I'm sure Mr. Ford wanted to create a good life—a good story—so he developed the assembly line to more efficiently manufacture cars. But there was a major *obstacle*; most people were too poor to purchase a car. Ford saw an *opportunity* within this difficulty and decided to pay his employees well so they could buy his cars.

Here is a strategy for you: when you face an obstacle, see it not as opposing you, but as guiding and re-routing you to a better direction and new opportunity. This is an optimistic thought that keeps you in the game until you figure out a new strategy. Brainstorm with other people. Ask the Universe to supply the answer during your sleep. Give yourself time so intuitive wisdom can find a new path. Purposefully create a better movie.

If you were raised in a home where most thoughts were pessimistic, you will need to re- train your mind—

change the computer programming—to make optimistic thoughts. One good strategy is to start your day with gratitude. Think of three people in your life to whom you are grateful. Think of three things for which you are grateful. From the small things, like a cup of coffee or green grass, to the wonderful, mysterious body you have that allows you to navigate in the world. Count your blessings. Acknowledge you are rich in health, or rich in friendships, or rich in a strong family. Finally, say "thank you." By sending out gratitude, you will receive it back.

Thomas was a client who grew up with an alcoholic dad who was in and out of jobs, and a co-dependent mother who allowed this harmful behavior to continue. The family life was chaotic and they were always poor. Thomas was the oldest sibling so he tried to keep peace in the house and food on the table.

As an adult, Thomas was married to a loving wife and had three children but experienced depressing and anxious thoughts. He didn't like his pessimistic perspective, so he came in for counseling. In my office, he would share things from his past and experience depressing thoughts. He would also share his negative predictions about work, and family, and would become anxious.

After telling me his childhood story and knowing I had heard him, he was open to a new way to understand and live his life. He realized that when his thoughts went to the past, he became depressed. When his thoughts went to the future, he became anxious. He learned how to stay in the present moment.

He was bright, competent, and had a good heart. Thomas realized if he kept his thoughts in the present moment, he did not become depressed or anxious and he could handle whatever crossed his path. He started the practice of seeing *opportunity in every difficulty*.

Let's see how Thomas's case fits with the three truths:

Truth #1: *Your thoughts create your reality.* Because of his childhood, it was understandable that Thomas had thoughts of scarcity and fear of not being able to take care of his family financially. Thomas changed these pessimistic views and created a new reality by keeping his thoughts in the present moment.

Truth #2: *There is no reality outside your interpretation of it.* Thomas's reality moved from fear of poverty and homelessness, to thinking and feeling that he would be able to take care of his family's needs, and even take some family vacations.

Truth #3: *You are not your thoughts.* Thomas's old thoughts of fear, poverty, and unemployment would cross his mind. He knew those thoughts appeared because of habit or because he felt depressed and anxious. He knew they were merely thoughts, so he let them go, moved into the present moment, embraced the thought he was competent, and felt peaceful and strong.

Jim Carrey's character in the movie *Dumb and Dumber* is interested in a beautiful woman. He asks her, "What are my chances?" She answers, "One in a million." He thinks about her response, and then says, "So you're telling me there's a chance. Yeah!" Carrey's humor is telling us to look for the light in the dark. That is a good movie. Work on increasing the positive instead of the negative. Create a good move—a good life. As Winston Churchill said, " ... see opportunity in every difficulty."

Reflections

1. Since everything begins with a thought, be aware of any pessimistic thoughts. See any obstacle as guiding and re-routing you

2. If you find yourself stuck in a particular situation, think like the little engine that could. Say to yourself, "I think I can. I think I can."

3. Start a gratitude journal. If you don't like to write, each morning say out loud three things for which you are grateful.

Chapter 4

D

"Peace is the result of retraining your mind to process life as it is, rather than as you think it should be."

*Wayne **D**yer*

Wayne Dyer, 1940-2015, was an international best-selling author of 30 books, philosopher, and motivational speaker. His first book, *Your Erroneous Zones* is one of the best selling books of all time, with an estimated 35 million copies sold.

Commonly used statements like, "It is what it is." "Let it be." "Let go and let God," help us retrain our thinking to accept life as it shows up. Most people resist accepting for a variety of reasons. One reason is because their ego mind judges the external event as negative. For example, a car that cuts you off in traffic, you tap the breaks to slow down, and your mind starts to resist. "He's a (expletive deleted). He shouldn't be driving. I'm going to tail him." You suffer for a period of time. For a moment it feels good and your ego mind justifies it. But the suffering continues.

Here is an example that raises the stakes. A parent receives a call from the school counselor because her 8-year-old child hit another boy on the playground. The mom's mind races. "That cannot be right. My son would never do that." She pauses. "What will the school administration think of me? Will other parents allow their children to play with my son?" Her mind continues to race. She thinks of how this will negatively impact her, and resists what the school reported. She suffers. Her negative energy will create more suffering for her child. She might never understand the lesson her son must learn.

Finally, an example that is more severe. The doctor tells the patient he has cancer. The immediate response is "This should not be happening to me." He becomes depressed, continues to go to medical appointments, but he has lost his fight.

Accepting what is, is not a passive, resigned attitude. It is a *retraining* of your *mind* so you have the freedom, flexibility, and clarity to figure out your next step in that specific adventure. If you find yourself behind a slow driver, watch your thoughts, do not buy into the judgmental ones, and create more productive thoughts. While being an observer of your thoughts, you could think, *Oh, there is that thought that I am this super important person and no one should slow me down.* That observation adds some humor which will loosen your tightly-wound mind. You can now have some fun with your thoughts. *I am going to lean into the levity of that thought, let go of it, and find peace in driving slower.* Your thoughts are becoming more productive. *Hey, someday I'm going to be the old man who isn't making the best decisions. Forgive him.* Finally, another productive thought: *I will also see when it's safe to switch lanes and travel closer to the speed limit.* If your child acts out at school, see the automatic self-oriented thoughts that play out in your mind. Create some distance from those thoughts. Don't buy into them. Retrain your mind and suspend judgment while you're driving to the school. Enter the school doors with an open mind to hear the facts to make the best decisions about your son.

Finally, it will be a practice to retrain your mind if you receive a diagnosis of cancer. Watch your thoughts and practice staying positive. (Re-read Chapter 3 and practice seeing the opportunity in this difficulty.) Say to yourself, "I will educate myself on the best way to re- claim my health. I am will find the best team of doctors. I am going to eat healthier. I will see my children get married." These thoughts, as Wayne Dyer said, are processing life as it is, rather than as you think it should be.

Everybody says they want to be happy, but few people want to do what it takes. If you sincerely have the goal of being happy, productive, and able to solve the problems that cross your path, you must trust in the way life unfolds. You must see the potential for health and healing in every life circumstance in the same way a psychologist sees this potential in every client. If a client didn't possess the potential for health and healing, what would be the point of talk therapy, medications, and therapeutic assignments?

Neale Donald Walsch, author of the series *Conversations with God*, wrote, "Mastery is not measured by the number of terrible things you eliminate from your life, but by the number of times you eliminate calling them terrible."

There are many reasons not to label circumstances as terrible. First, you lose your peace of mind. Second, it's exhausting to resist life. It's like pushing a boulder up a hill, only to have it roll down and have to push it up again. Third, how do you know it's terrible? It is your ego mind reacting. For example, a local businessman had a national competitor come to his town. He didn't label it terrible. He created a niche market for himself and is making more money than before. What about the passenger who was late and missed boarding the Titanic; was that terrible?

A significant other breaks up with you. After the heartache, you see a different side to him/her, which you were blind to before the breakup. In time, you are grateful for not investing more time in that relationship.

You realize you are in a dead-end job. You don't see that as terrible, and you continue to fulfill your job responsibilities. But you don't waste energy in the negativity because you are investing your efforts in a start-up business or looking for a new job.

For most parents, when a child leaves adolescence, it is difficult for the parent to let go and let the child enter adulthood on his/her own. It was difficult for me. When one of my children was taking a path that I would not have voted for, I struggled and suffered. During this time a friend asked me about our children and I reported on this child's decisions and how I was struggling with it. He reflected to me that I must be exhausted. I told him I was, and then asked, "How did you know?" He said it is exhausting whenever one resists life. The light bulb went on for me. I thought I knew what was right and did not trust God and my young adult child. I practiced letting go and over time felt better and had more energy. As Wayne Dyer suggests, I retrained my mind to process life as it is, rather than as I thought it should be.

A couple in their late 40's came to my office. Their problem was that their only child, an 18-year-old son, had told them he was gay. They were afraid their son would be unhappy because of the negative views society holds about gays.

I asked about their son, and they both said he was well-adjusted, happy, and successful at school. He had never had a girlfriend, which now made sense, but he had a wide social circle of friends. I asked them why they thought these wonderful traits would change because their son was gay. They said there is rampant discrimination, and their 18-year-old had no idea what the real world was like.

Let's see how these parents' case fits in the three truths:

Truth #1: *Your thoughts create your reality.* The parents, who were in their late 40s, had grown up during a time when there was hostility toward homosexuals and discrimination was widespread. By 2018, the societal perspectives had changed significantly. Same sex marriage was legal, gay people were running for national office, and there was a much wider acceptance of different sexual orientations. We spent many sessions looking at their thoughts and how they created fear. They did not want to live in fear, so creating new paradigms (thoughts), talking with their son and realizing he was not living in fear, helped move them to a more productive way to live with this new reality.

Truth #2: *There is no reality outside your interpretation of it.* The parents came into my office certain of the fact that their child would be unhappy, judged, and stuck in life because of his sexuality. This interpretation was unhealthy and unproductive. They were the ones who were unhappy and stuck in life. By understanding the change in society and more fully understanding their son, their thoughts changed, which caused their reality to change, and they were more trusting that their son would continue to be happy as an adult.

Truth #3: *You are not your thoughts.* The parents didn't realize their cultural experiences had created thoughts of fear. The fear felt real to them, so they assumed the fears were real. They came to realize their fear had come from their thoughts. Through counseling, talking with other people, and most importantly, talking with their son, they realized that their fear was based on their thoughts. They created new thoughts that helped guide them to a new roadmap.

Paul McCartney sings "Whisper words of wisdom, let it be." When something that is different than you think it should be happens, and is beyond your control, I suggest you whisper, speak, or yell "Let it be." Whatever has happened in your life, it has happened. It is what it is. Now, if you want to change something, and it is within your sphere of influence, communicate and try to change it. But don't resist "what is." Let it be. Then you will not have emotional chaos that harms your effort to create productive change.

Reflections

1. Draw a circle, and inside the circle write "My circle of acceptance." Now, name something in your life that you are resisting. Write that down outside your circle of acceptance. Now draw a bigger circle that includes what was outside. How does it feel to widen the circle of what you will accept? What will you do differently?

2. Name something that you have labeled terrible. Practice not calling it terrible. You may call it unhealthy or unproductive. Practice being a change agent to that which you think is unhealthy and unproductive. If the other person doesn't want to change, your change will be to accept and create healthy boundaries.

3. Picture yourself moving toward a healthier and happier way of living in the world. What old thoughts would you let go of to become that picture of well-being? Where do you need to retrain your mind so you can process life as it is?

Chapter 5

E

*"We cannot solve our problems with the same
thinking we used when we created them."*

Albert Einstein

Einstein was a theoretical physicist who developed the
theory of relativity. He received the 1921 Nobel Prize in
Physics for his discovery which led to the development of
quantum theory. Einstein was Time Magazine's Person of
the 20th Century.

The quote above is powerful for many reasons.
First, as was stated in the Introduction, everything starts
with a thought. Thoughts then create feelings, which
coupled together, form our behaviors. Einstein is saying our
thinking created our problems, and we can't continue to
think that specific way if we want to solve that exact
problem. We have to go back to the beginning step and
change our *thoughts.*
Second, Einstein is stating that *we* created our
problems. We cannot blame someone else. We created our
reality with our thoughts. If we want to solve the problem,
we have to look inward and discern what new thought(s),
which lead to a new behavior, might solve the problem.

A couple came to my office because of their
adolescent son, Alex. His grades had dropped to C's, D's
and F's. I asked the parents many questions about their

son's history and the parenting styles that had worked and not worked with Alex.

The husband started talking to his wife Amy: "You are way too easy on him. He walks all over you. Alex needs to be grounded and not see daylight until he gets his grades up!" The wife fired back: "You are way too strict with Alex. He's rebelling against your authority. He needs a dad not a drill sergeant."

Upon examination of their thought processes, mom admitted to these thoughts on her parenting style with Alex: "I want to be his friend," and "My parents were way too strict with me, and I vowed I would not be that way with my children." The dad's thoughts on parenting were; "My children should obey me. When I see my wife being too loose with Alex, I feel like I need to really tighten up the ship."

I drew a continuum and labeled the ends "too loose," and "too tight." They both smiled because they knew where each of them landed on the continuum. I then drew a two inch oval in the middle. I reflected to them that if the mom continued to be too lax with her parenting style, the problems would continue. If the dad continued to be too strict, the problems would continue. With awareness that their parenting styles were at the extreme end of the same continuum, they both agreed to change their thinking on how to parent and come more to the middle. The mom agreed to let go of the idea of wanting to be Alex's friend, and give consequences if grades fell below a certain level. The dad agreed to let go of the thoughts of wanting unquestioned obedience and he agreed to create thoughts that would lead him to spend time with Alex, ask open-ended questions, and be more supportive.

Each parent's specific thoughts on how to parent Alex created problems. They exacerbated the problem by attaching more firmly with these thoughts. That "same thinking" did not solve the problem. Only by changing their thoughts, which led to a more balanced method of parenting, did the problem get resolved.

People with anger problems tend to have thoughts that tell them that people are trying to harm or control them in some way. People with co-dependency problems tend to have thoughts of needing to fix people. Anxious people tend to have worrisome thoughts about the future. People who are perfectionists have thoughts of impossibly high standards. All these people learned these ways of thinking somewhere in their life journey. They think these thoughts are "correct" so they continue thinking this way. Sadly, their problems continue.

The good news is if that you learned this, you can unlearn it and learn a healthier and more productive way of thinking. The person with anger problems can learn to think that his boss is not out to get him. The boss might be in a bad mood or following orders from *his* boss. The person who thinks in a co-dependent way can learn new ways of thinking about relationships. Thoughts of staying independent and not trying to fix others can guide her. The anxious person can learn how to think only about the present moment. He can learn ways to stay grounded and take care of what is right in front of him. Perfectionists can learn to create thoughts about healthy and more typical standards. They can repeat the thought, "This is good enough," instead of over-working projects.

Carol, a full professor at the University of Nebraska, came into my office. She said that anxiety was getting the best of her. She said the anxiety had started in high school when she realized "grades mattered." Her Master's thesis almost landed her in the hospital because she was always "scribbling in the margins about how the paper could be better." She gave a weak smile and said she didn't want to talk about her Ph.D. experience

I asked Carol if perfectionism was an issue in her life. She answered yes, and asked me how I knew. I said, "Your answers to my questions gave it away." She became a little defensive. "I described hard work. And I pride myself on my work ethic."

Of course I agreed. We talked about the power of our thoughts. I asked Carol whether it was as if steroids powered her thoughts on work.

She smiled again, nodded her head, and then asked if this caused her anxiety.

I answered by asking another question: "Do you think your work is good, but always double down to make it a bit better?"

She answered, "Yes, and it drives me crazy." Emotions filled her eyes. "I am open to changing that."

This was the key to doing good work in my office and practicing new ways of thinking and acting at work.

Let's see how Carol's case fits with the three truths:

Truth #1: *Your thoughts create your reality.* Carol's thoughts of *work hard* and *everything can be made incrementally better* were a problem for her. Carol realized that her thoughts, *I don't believe my work is that good,* and *I'm one semester away from being fired* created a hellish reality her. When Carol changed her thoughts to *I'm competent and if the University wants to fire me or they shut down my department, I will find another good paying job.* This reduced her anxiety to the normal amount of butterflies one has before making a pitch to the National Endowment for a research project.

Truth #2: *There is no reality outside your interpretation of it.* Carol created an anxiety-filled reality with her perfectionist thoughts. She created even more anxiety when her thoughts drove her to believe that her work was never good enough. After she learned new strategies, she went back to the same building on campus, interacted with the same people, but created a different reality with her thoughts. Her thoughts allowed her to accept the products of her work, which led to a more peaceful reality.

Truth #3: *You are not your thoughts.* After a couple of sessions, I asked Carol a question to see if she understood the concept of thoughts. "Carol, which one of these statements is you. 'I am a hard worker that is never quite satisfied with my results,' or 'I am a hard worker who is seeking balance with my expectations of my results.' With a wry smile she answered "Good pop quiz, Pete. You should be a professor. The answer is neither. They are merely thoughts that guide me on which behavior I choose."

Carol realized her thought *I am anxious* was not true. Her new language was *I am experiencing anxiety.* This created some distance between her thoughts and her self-concept. She understood that anxiety comes and goes—it is not who she is.

Martha Beck wrote in *Steering By Starlight,* "The process of weakening a false thought is a little like losing a baby tooth; at first, you may only feel a tiny bit of 'give,' a slight wiggle away from rigid belief and constant emotional pain. But as the mind turns its energy to dis- proving a painful thought, rather than proving it over and over again, the wiggling becomes more pronounced. You feel freer and freer, until one day you forget you ever believed something that is now obviously untrue."

Reflections

1. Name a problem in your life. Brainstorm new ways of thinking about the solution. Ask others how they would think about solving the problem. Journal about what new behaviors would come from these new thoughts.
2. Your parents did the best they could. They still fell short. Name something unhealthy you learned from your childhood. Now, state to yourself a new, healthier way to think about that specific dynamic. Practice living that new way of thinking.
3. Change your language with your growth area. Your new language includes "I am" statements: "I am experiencing anxiety. I am experiencing perfectionism. I am experiencing feeling sad."

Chapter 6

Γ

"Everything can be taken from a man but one thing: the last of human freedoms—to choose one's attitude in any given set of circumstances, to choose one's own way."

Viktor Frankl

Frankl was a Jew from Austria, a psychiatrist, and a Holocaust survivor. While he was a concentration camp inmate, he discovered the importance of finding meaning in everything he experienced. His popular book, *Man's Search for Meaning,* was originally titled, *Saying Yes to Life in Spite of Everything.*

I teach one night a week at a local university. This quarter the class is called Life Span Development. I was thinking of how to write about Frankl's quote, and the textbook for this class had two interesting and pertinent points. In the Middle Adulthood chapter, this jumped out at me: "The stress and coping paradigm views stress not as an environmental stimulus or as a response, but as the interaction of a *thinking* person and an event. How we interpret an event such as being stuck in traffic is what matters, not the event itself or what we do in response to it." (Lazarus 1984).

The next week, we were covering death and dying in Later Adulthood. This is what jumped out at me: "It is how a person *interprets* a loss, rather than the event itself, that causes depression In this approach, internal *belief* systems, or what one tells oneself about why certain things are happening are emphasized as the cause of depression." (Segal, et al., 2011).

Frankl states that " ... the last of human freedoms (is to) chose one's attitude ... " For example, during middle adulthood when we might have a huge workload, including raising children, working hard as a provider, volunteering at church or a local non-profit, and trying to find some recreational fun, our attitude determines whether we experience stress.

During later adulthood, it is inevitable that a spouse and friends will die. A couple of dearly loved pets will have passed away. One could interpret these losses as depressing. But research shows—and Frankl states—that one's internal belief system and one's attitude determines if sadness regresses into depression.

In the Introduction, I wrote that your conditions do not lead inevitably to suffering. It is your perspective on the conditions that can lead to suffering. Frankl also writes, "It is not freedom from conditions, but it is freedom to take a stand toward the conditions." It is the ability to see if your thoughts are moving toward being aversive or judgmental to the condition. Then, letting go of those non-productive thoughts, and changing them to productive thoughts of purposeful communication, resolving conflicts or forgiveness.

Frankl went on to write, "Every human being has the freedom to change at any instant." Yes! You are free to change your thoughts—change your attitude—to acceptance, tolerance, and compassionate boundary setting, at any instant. This is how your mind can be a wonderful servant.

Paul was a client who had been married for 29 years. He grew up in a dysfunctional home where his mother was physically bigger than his father and wielded more emotional power. The mother would slap her husband and Paul when she lost her temper. Paul could never measure up to his mom's expectations, and his dad never intervened and also never said any kind words to his son.

Paul repeated this childhood pattern and married a woman who was similar to his mom. He made the marriage work by never fighting back and by giving in to her constant demands. He never saw it coming when his wife had an affair and left Paul for a man three states away. Paul came to my office depressed. After a couple of sessions, he realized that the depression came from childhood trauma and his marriage. He had a hopeless attitude toward life, relationships, and getting better.

We unpacked the similarities between his wife and his mother. Paul realized that he had learned from his childhood that women were distant and emotionally abusive. He also learned that men should be weak and not stand up to people in power.

Frankl talked about the importance of attitude. Attitude is a mental and emotional position with regard to a person or thing. Paul and I talked about his "mental position"—his thinking—with regard to his mom, dad, and soon to be ex-wife. When Paul was a child, he had limited power, so he learned that he had to take the emotional abuse. Paul kept that "mental position" when he was an adult and married. Our therapy was about unlearning those attitudes, and learning new attitudes of self-worth, effective communication, and healthy boundaries. These new attitudes created a more positive outlook for Paul. The depression lifted, Paul felt empowered to talk to his boss about an age-old issue. He wasn't ready to date, but he could see himself entering that world someday.

Let's see how Paul's case fits into the three truths:

Truth #1: *Your thoughts create your reality.* Paul's thoughts were negative toward himself and toward life .

51

Because of these negative thoughts, his reality included abuse, neglect, and despair. Paul learned in therapy that he could think about people and things in a new way. He learned how to *think* that he deserved respect from himself and others. He learned to *think* differently about communication, and that he could ask for what he needed. He learned that it's okay to *think* about himself, take care of himself, and set achievable goals for the life he wanted. These thoughts created an entirely different reality of love, growth, mutual respect and hope.

Truth #2: *There is no reality outside your interpretation of it.* Most people would interpret Paul's childhood as abusive and believe that Child Protective Services should have been called in to protect him. As a child, Paul did not know any better, and his interpretation of the abuse was that he was doing things wrong. As an adult, his interpretation of his marriage was that his wife's behaviors were normal. He even felt relief that he wasn't being hit by his wife. Paul learned in therapy that he could interpret relationships differently. He learned that he was a good person, that life could be friendly, and that he could be in a relationship where each person genuinely cared about the other's welfare.

Truth #3: *You are not your thoughts.* If Paul were his thoughts, his life would have been destined to be unhealthy and filled with toxic people. Paul learned that he could change his attitude, and practiced creating new, healthier thoughts. Paul's life was, as Frankl said, "changed in an instant." (Or, possibly after many counseling sessions.)

Paulo Coelho, the Brazilian novelist, best known for his novel *The Alchemist,* wrote, "You have two choices, to control your mind or to let your mind control you." All of us, at certain times, allow our minds to control us. We forget that we can "choose (our) attitude in any given set of circumstance." During this time of forgetting, we become victims, and lash out at others or ourselves. If we are aware when our mind creates unproductive thoughts, we can use our practices of letting those thoughts go, and create healthier and more productive thoughts.

Reflections

1. If you feel you've lost your freedom in a particular situation, take a step back, look at your attitude, and create new thoughts that will lead you to a more peaceful existence.
2. To varying degrees, we are all products of our childhood. Be a scientist and examine the thinking processes that were taught and modeled to you. Change the thoughts that lead you to unhealthy ways of being in the world.
3. When you are in a foul mood, you have allowed your mind to control you. (The mind is a terrible master.) Get back in the driver's seat and watch your negative, toxic, judgmental thoughts. Smile and say that you are going to control your mind and create healthier thoughts. (The mind is a wonderful servant.)

Chapter 7

G

"If I have the belief that I can do it, I shall surely acquire the capacity to do it even if I may not have it at the beginning."

Mahatma Gandhi

Mohandas Gandhi was an activist who was the leader of the Indian independence movement against Great Britain. Gandhi's non-violent, civil disobedience tactics helped lead India to its independence and inspired civil rights movements around the world. Because of his accomplishments and loving nature, he was given the title Mahatma, or Great Soul.

A Christian teaching challenges us to have faith like a child. Why like a child? One reason is because children have not yet created self-defeating beliefs. For example, even though young children have not fully developed the skill of walking, children *believe* they can walk. When toddlers fall, they do not berate themselves or go into stinkin' thinkin'. They *believe* they can *acquire the capacity* to do it, even though they have fallen. They keep picking themselves up and practicing the skill of walking.

Many adults lose this faith and belief in themselves. After "falling," they stop believing they can continue an exercise program. They stop believing they should apply for a promotion. They stop believing they can resolve problems with their spouse or significant other.

Henry Ford said, "If you think you can or you think you can't, you're right." (This quote is also used in Chapter 3. It is so powerful and pertinent, it bears repeating.) If I may use multiple car metaphors, our belief system is the engine that powers our life. It is the chassis that we sit in all day. It is the gear that allows us to get us out of a rut or keeps our wheels spinning. It is critical that we bring to the light our belief systems, because they are the reason why we are in a healthy or unhealthy place.

Initially, we consciously and unconsciously adopt our belief systems from our family of origin. The older we get, we also unconsciously and consciously form our belief systems through our work environment, friends, religious organizations, media, and our own personal insight about how we want to live in the world.

Belief systems are interconnected. For example, you might have learned the belief system from your family that others can't be trusted and you must take care of just yourself. You start dating someone who attends church. You attend services with him or her and learn that it is important to help those who are less fortunate and to give freely to the poor and hungry. Your significant other donates to the red kettle in front of the grocery store and wants you to serve meals at the local food kitchen. These two belief systems are incongruent and are colliding. You're being forced to question an early belief system. Which one will you adopt and act upon?

Sometimes it takes time to process the information from a new belief system. It is important to talk about the conflict you are feeling. Ask questions and practice living the new belief system to see how it feels. Eventually your old unhealthy belief system will lose power as your new belief system begins to guide you. Personal growth occurs when we allow the integration of a healthy new belief system We could also do the opposite and, because of external negative factors, allow the integration of an unhealthy belief system. We could become more self-defeating, racist, homophobic, or sexist.

As parents, we tell our teenagers, "You are who you hang out with." Parents want their adolescent children to hang with peers who have healthy belief systems. Unhealthy belief systems can lead to teenage pregnancy, drug and alcohol use, and other undesirable behaviors. As adults, this is true for us also. Making friends and hanging out with co-workers who have healthy belief systems will help you live a more productive, happier life.

Early in my counseling career, I had a court-ordered client. Nan was 20 years old and became pregnant during her senior year of high school. The child's father was completely absent, and she became overwhelmed so she dropped out of school. Her child was now two years old, and Nan spanked him so hard and often, it created bruises on the back of the toddler's legs and buttocks. Nan told me she was a good parent. She loved her son and wanted what was best for him. She was earnest in her statements, and it was obvious that she thought she was a good mother.

During our sessions, Nan talked often about her child's negative behaviors. She showed more disapproval of her child than approval. The behaviors Nan was referring to were typical two-year-old behaviors. I reflected to Nan that toddlers explore, get into things, strive for autonomy, and push boundaries. She nodded, but then added, "You don't know my child."

Nan was not conscious of the belief system she had of her child and how that guided her parenting style. Nan could not admit she had negative feelings toward the child. Getting pregnant and then having the child's father take no responsibility had changed her perspective on men and overwhelmed her to the point where she didn't finish high school. She saw her life as forever changed in a negative way. She unconsciously blamed her child.

Nan did not recognize the thoughts that rejected her child because she had not yet admitted her negative beliefs about being a parent. She looked for aggressive acts by her son and saw typical behaviors as oppositional and negative. Since "good parents" try to help their child change these unhealthy behaviors, she unconsciously perceived much of her child's behavior as bad and punished him accordingly.

The goals of our counseling sessions were to stop the abusive behaviors and help Nan be conscious of her negative belief systems on parenting, men, her son, and her life that had changed drastically. Once we brought these beliefs into the light, I reflected that it would be typical for a young, single mom who had been abandoned by the child's father to have these negative thoughts. But it is vitally important to "see" these thoughts, let them go, and not act on them. Nan started to change the beliefs she held against her child. She accepted the typical two- ear-old behaviors and played with him, kept him safe, and loved him no matter what. She started to "acquire the capacity to do it (parent well) even if (she) may not have it at the beginning."

Let's see how's case fits these three truths:

Truth #1: *Your thoughts create your reality.* Nan's case is a good example of the power of unconscious thoughts. She could not admit that she had negative thoughts about her child. It would be very difficult to admit—make conscious—the thought that you dislike your child because of how he changed your life. Those unproductive thoughts are present, have power, and will be manifested. Nan acted them out by looking for negative behaviors in her son. Her reality was constantly dark and full of anger. Once Nan realized her unhealthy belief systems, she changed her thoughts toward her child which created a lighter and happier environment.

Truth #2: *There is no reality outside your interpretation of it.* The daycare provider who saw the bruises interpreted that reality and called Child Protective Services. The judge interpreted Nan's behaviors as a need for a multifaceted intervention. Initially, Nan interpreted the reality of the bruises as good parenting which would change the little boy's behaviors. Later, she changed her thoughts about her child and a more loving reality was created.

Truth #3: *You are not your thoughts.* Nan's thoughts before she become pregnant were typical adolescent thoughts. She complained about homework, wanted to hang out with friends, and thought she had fallen in love and met the man of her dreams. Nan's life and her thoughts took a drastic turn as an eighteen-year-old. When she realized she was pregnant, her thoughts were more depressing and full of fear. When her child was born and through age two, her thoughts became darker which led to abusive behavior. These three different scenarios—Nan as carefree teenager, Nan as pregnant girl, Nan as harried mom—led Nan to have certain thoughts that led to particular behaviors. Which one is the true Nan? None of them. They were merely three acts in the play called Nan. The script for each play was the thoughts which led to the behaviors and emotional states.

Alan Cohen, author of 27 inspirational books, said, "All limits exist only in thought, and that is where they are overcome." With practice, motivation, and perseverance, you can change your thinking, increase your emotional intelligence, and learn new behaviors to overcome limits and *acquire the capacity* to live a more productive, happier life.

Reflections

1. Name a new belief system that you are beginning to acquire the capacity to follow. Where are you on the continuum of full integration? How will your life be better when you do?
2. I am practicing a new belief in which I embrace change and it is my friend. It is colliding with my belief that I like things to say the same. What are two belief systems that are colliding in your life? How are you managing the discomfort.
3. Name a three-act play in your life. You are currently living in Act 2. What do you want to happen in Act 3? Start writing that script and live it.

Chapter 8

H

"I don't fix my problems. I fix my thinking then problems fix themselves."

*Louise **Hay***

Louise Hay was an author of 18 books on healing techniques and positive psychology. In 1988, she opened her publishing company Hay House. She created the Hay Foundation to support organizations that enhance the quality of life for people, animals, and the environment.

      I believe the earth is a big school house. We are here to learn lessons. If we learn our lessons, life becomes easier, and we experience more happiness. If we don't learn our lessons, life becomes more difficult, and we experience more anger, anxiety, or depression.

      Your life lesson curriculum always begins with some circumstance in your external world. Your boss treats you poorly. Your spouse isn't fully honoring you. Your friends don't respect you the way you think they should. You keep running out of money.

      Our habit is to identify with the thought that judges the external events in our life. "My husband should have planned a better trip for our anniversary." "My friend should have written a thank- you letter." "My checkbook has a negative balance. I hate money!" "Why does it have to rain on my day off?" When we think this way—blame external conditions—we are more likely not to learn our life lessons, because we are not examining how we are thinking about that external circumstances.

Your thoughts can be directed to the outside world or toward you and your life lessons. Your thoughts can be full of resistance or they can accept "what is," and discover your life lesson so that you don't continue to experience the unhealthy or uncomfortable circumstance.

Albert Einstein is quoted as saying that the most important question a person can ask is: Is the Universe a friendly or hostile place? What do you believe? Is the Universe friendly? Hostile? Or a combination of the two?

Most people believe it is a combination of the two. The result of this belief is that they are happy when they agree with what happens in the external world, and unhappy when they don't agree.

I believe the Universe is friendly. When something agitating, uncomfortable, or surprising happens in my world, the first question I ask myself is, "What is my life lesson?" I don't *fix the problem. I fix my thinking.* I contemplate, ask trusted people, and try to discern a new way of looking at the "problem." I then change my thinking to learn my life lesson and reduce the suffering that accompanies the "problem."

One way to discern your life lessons is to realize that your mind is a mirror. For example, if you saw a dirty face and messy hair in a mirror, you might feel surprise and distaste. You would see the folly if you tried to tidy up the image by washing the mirror. You know the mirror is reflective and designed to show you yourself. You understand that you have to change yourself. Similarly, life is designed to reflect your belief systems to you. For example, if you keep running out of money, you probably have a belief system of scarcity. If you keep attracting people who treat you poorly, you probably think poorly of yourself. If you believe people will like you, you probably like yourself. If life keeps working out for you, you probably are learning your life lessons and have a belief system that the Universe is friendly.

Ian grew up in a household of conflict. His father was passive, and his mom angry and usually in an emotional disagreement with someone. Ian often saw his mom arguing with his dad and maternal grandparents. As a young child, Ian remembered climbing under the kitchen table to escape his mom's yelling. He remembers lying in bed at night and hearing fights between mom and dad. Ian often felt alone because most of his parents' attention was directed to perceived conflicts with others.

Ian married a woman who had a chip on her shoulder and often felt slighted by others. Ian could never measure up to his wife's expectations and was often berated by her. He came into my office feeling overwhelmed and depressed.

I wanted Ian to understand how his childhood experiences influenced his choice of a wife. "Ian," I asked, "is there any similarity between your current situation at home and the home you grew up in?"

He waited a second. "Yes, they are both full of conflict."

"Do you think you have a belief system that negativity and win-lose conflicts are part of home life?"

He waited another second. "I hate to say this, but yeah, that's what I know."

"Ian, are you here because you want to change that?"

He sat up. "Yes!" he said emphatically. "Can that be done?"

"Yes. We are going to work on creating a new belief system for you about your ideal home. If you change your thoughts, I believe your problems will be resolved."

Our work centered on *fixing* two belief systems. The first was the belief that home life was always going to be negative and life draining. The second belief system that Ian had to *fix* was that there was no potential life partner who would love him for who he is. Through time, he incrementally changed his thoughts to believe that home life could be full of love and compassion. With conscious practices and trying unsuccessfully to resolve conflicts with his wife, he left her and is now dating a woman who loves Ian and expresses to him how wonderful he is. Life is now mirroring to Ian his new belief about himself: I am a good guy and deserve to be treated fairly.

Let's see how's case fits these three truths:

Truth #1: *Your thoughts create your reality.* When I first met Ian, his thoughts created a toxic reality at home. When Ian changed his thoughts about himself and home, his reality was changed to a more loving existence.

Truth #2: *There is no reality outside your interpretation of it.* Ian believed that he deserved negative people in his life. He believed that he would always fall short of his wife's expectations. Once Ian changed his thoughts about himself, he created a new reality where healthy communication, acceptance, and love existed.

Truth #3: *You are not your thoughts.* Luckily for Ian, he was not the person his wife and mother reflected to him. With lots of awareness and practice, Ian started blooming into the kind, articulate, hardworking person that he wanted to be.

C.S. Lewis, the author of more than 30 books, said, "You can't go back and change the beginning, but you can start where you are and change the ending." Circumstances do not dictate one's destiny. How one thinks about the circumstances determines the quality of one's life. Everything starts with a thought. Practice directing your first thought to yourself. Practice changing your thought about what life is reflecting to you. It's not about the mirror—life—it's about your thinking.

Reflections

1. Name a "problem" in your life. Your current thinking has not resolved that "problem" because you are probably complaining about the external circumstances. Now "fix" that problem by only thinking about what *you* will do about it. Practice that new awareness and monitor it to see how you now participate with that issue.

2. Life mirrors your belief systems. What would you like life to mirror back to you? Take time to discern what new thoughts you need to create to change your external world and what it mirrors back to you.

3. How can you "start where you are and change the ending" to a specific life situation?

Chapter 9

I

"If what you are thinking doesn't make you feel good, change that thought. Bad cannot bother you unless you are available."

Iyanla Vanzant

Iyanla is an American inspirational speaker and author. She appeared many times on the Oprah Winfrey show and had her own talk show.

"Bad cannot bother you unless you are available." Usually, unhappiness, rejection, despair, and suffering show up if we think that way about ourselves, others, or our life circumstances. As I've said in previous chapters, nearly everyone wants to be happy. Most people would prefer not to suffer. Then why do we continue to experience these harmful and wounding states of being? I believe it's because we do not fully realize that our happiness does not depend on our external life conditions. Our happiness depends on our internal thought processes about these conditions. I also believe we experience these detrimental states because we are not disciplined in watching our thoughts, letting go of judgmental ones, and creating healthier thoughts.

The Buddhist tradition teaches that there are the Five Hindrances to living in a peaceful state. These hindrances are negative mental states that make us available to the "bad." The first hindrance is our thoughts of desire. This can be tied to the happiness we think we will derive through the five senses. We think we will be happy if we eat more chocolate. We think we will be more fulfilled if we find another sexual partner. We think we will be more accepted if we buy a sportier car or the latest fashion. If you desire none of these things, this might sound like foolishness to you. But when you succumb to thoughts of desire, they feel like the antidote to your loneliness, low self-esteem, or unhappiness. We all know that these things may bring short-term pleasure, but they definitely do not bring long-term happiness. In fact, in time, they create more "bad" and suffering for us.

The second hindrance is ill-will. This can be tied to our thoughts of rejecting our life conditions. Thoughts of hatred, hostility, and resentment will follow not accepting life as it shows up. We might initially feel better after complaining and lamenting about what our friend did, or how the traffic was that morning, or our workload, but this reinforces judgmental thinking and then life conditions have power over us. We must practice compassion and acceptance and then the "bad" will not find us, and we will live more peacefully.

The third hindrance is sloth and boredom. This is when we oppose anything wholesome . We experience inertia, lack of energy, and see the monotony in our life. Since we are not engaged in a healthy activity, our mind tends to move toward the unhealthy, and the "bad" will find us. A child may experience this and negative behaviors will occur. A parent will step in and find an activity for the child to do and this hindrance disappears. We need to do the same. Create forward motion in your life. Take a walk. Read a book. Create a new hobby.

The fourth hindrance is restlessness and worry. The Buddhists call this monkey mind; always jumping and swinging to the next branch. Never sitting still or relaxing into the moment or the day. This is caused by looking only outward and seeing the negative that needs to be fixed. The "bad" will find you because you are fault finding and want to fix it or to move on to something you think will be better. The antidote is to practice being contented. Look for things, small to big things, for which to be grateful. There also might be a good reason for your restlessness. Maybe you have an unresolved conflict with someone. Change your thinking, communicate, and try to work out the problem.

The fifth hindrance is doubt. "Am I doing the right thing?" "Do I have the ability?" "Can I trust this person?" These questions of doubt will allow the "bad" to find you because you are disheartened and not going forward on your journey. Talk to a trusted person or professional about your doubts. Seek clarity on your current situation and how to move forward. Create a good map where the destination is wholesome.

Jack was a single, handsome 28-year-old who dated beautiful women and had many sexual partners. He came to my office because he truly loved his girlfriend of two years, but he had not asked her to marry him. He was afraid that he might find another more beautiful or sexually pleasing woman. His hindrance of desire was creating conflict with his girlfriend and strife in his life.

Jack was open and honest with me and said that he didn't want to hurt his girlfriend. All his other friends were married and some already had children. Jack shared that he wanted to settle down but "I know myself—I can be a male whore. There are so many beautiful women, and I might take one back to my apartment some night."

I complimented Jack on knowing himself. I reflected to him that he really knew his thoughts of desire which led him to have many sexual partners. He gave me a perplexed look so I further explained. "Your thoughts lead you to have sex with many women. If you became more conscious of those thoughts of desire, let go of them, and create other thoughts that could lead you to 'settle down.'"

I waited a moment to let that soak in. I continued, "You are not a male whore. You may have acted like a male whore, but the true Jack is not a male whore. You merely allowed your thoughts to drive you."

"How do I let go of those thoughts?" he asked.

I thought for a moment. "If my office was on the top floor of a 10 story building, would you have thoughts of getting to the roof so you could jump off?"

"No."

"Of course not. You don't even give yourself the option of jumping off the building. The outcome will be bad." I paused. "How about using this same thinking strategy with having sex with other women? You will obviously see other women—like you see the roof of this building. You don't give yourself the option of turning on the charm, buying her a drink, and taking her home."

He gave me a half smile. "You're saying it's as simple as watching my sexual thoughts, letting them go, not buying into them, and I'll be more comfortable settling down with my girlfriend?"

"Yes," I answered.

The coin dropped. "That feels good."

"Do you think you can commit to your girlfriend?"

"Right now, yes."

"That's because your current thought is, 'It is not an option to be with another woman.'"

"Yes. And if that wanes in the future, I'll think of a 10 story building. It is not an option to jump from it. It is not an option to be with another woman." Jack learned to "change that thought." With practice, "bad" would not bother him because he was not available.

Truth #1: *Your thoughts create your reality.* Jack had thoughts about how the sexual grass was always greener. He changed those to thoughts of knowing that his girlfriend was ideal for him. He used the thought, "It is not an option to be with another woman," to create the new reality.

Truth #2: *There is no reality outside your interpretation of it.* Jack came in for counseling because he didn't see any way out of the reality of being sexually active with other women. He left counseling with a new reality of staying true to his girlfriend.

Truth #3: *You are not your thoughts.* If Jack were his thoughts, he was destined to never settle down and continue to be a "male whore."

Anne Lamott, author of 19 books said, "My coming to faith did not start with a leap but rather a series of staggers from what seemed like one safe place to another. Like lily pads, round and green, those places summoned and they held me up while I grew. Each prepared me for the next leap on which I would land, and in this way I moved across the swamp of doubt and fear." Marshal mental energy to change your thoughts, which will help you land in an emotionally safer place. Garner some more strength, take calculated risks to stay away from the Five Hindrances. Take charge of your life and decide not to allow "bad" to bother you. Change your thoughts, which will change your actions, to a life that is happier, lighter, and more productive. Your mind will no longer be a terrible master. It will be a wonderful servant.

Reflections

1. Where in your life is "bad" finding you? Figure out what thought is creating that. Change your thought.
2. Which of the Five Hindrances is your most common negative mental state? Give yourself permission to

let go of those thoughts and create healthier thoughts.

3. If your default mode is to justify feeling bad because of some habitual way of thinking, be honest with yourself and ask whether you really want to feel good, or do you want to continue to feel bad? Your rational mind will say "feel good." Your ego mind doesn't want to change and will continue to make you feel bad. Write or talk about this process.

Chapter 10

J

"It is done unto you as you believe."
Jesus

Christians see Jesus as the Son of God. Jews see him as a teacher. Muslims see him as a prophet. This scripture is the Good News translation of Matthew 9:29.
(I explain Jesus this way to further illustrate that *there is no reality outside your interpretation of it.* A person as powerful and wide-known as Jesus is interpreted three different ways by three different global religions.)

I introduce to you three stories that are manifestations of many clients. These stories are on a spectrum of unproductive to productive.

Deborah was raised by an alcoholic father and emotionally absent mother. When her dad came home drunk, her home life was chaotic. Since her mom did nothing about it, she *believed* it was her job to fix her dad. As an adult, she repeated her childhood experience and gravitated to what she knew. She married an alcoholic because she *believed* it was her job to fix him. Her life continued to be chaotic. It was "done unto" her as she believed.

Eddie was raised in a lower middle class home. Both dad and mom worked hard. Dad did not finish high school and mom earned a GED. The family never ate in restaurants, did not take vacations, and Eddie had to buy his own clothes during his adolescence. Eddie *believed* that living paycheck to paycheck and experiencing scarcity were truths of life. As an adult, Eddie did not pursue more education after high school, took a job where his dad worked, and *believed* that was as good as it would get. It was "done unto" him as he believed.

Steven was raised in a supportive home with two older brothers. The older brothers were star athletes and Steven *believed* if he worked hard enough, he could be as successful as they were. As an adult, he was competitive and *believed* he would be successful in every calculated risk he took. He became a successful businessman and civic-minded citizen. It was "done unto" him as he believed.

These three examples show how your thoughts—your beliefs—create your reality. Deborah, Steven, and Eddie learned specific things during their childhoods and believed them to be truths. Most of us do the same thing. A broader and more foundational way to look at this dynamic of creating your reality is from a global perspective. For example, what are your beliefs about life? How is the Universe designed? Is it a friendly place, a hostile place, or a combination of the two?

In my experience, most people believe the Universe is both friendly and hostile. What is "done unto" one who believes this? If life conditions are smooth and beneficial, one is happy If life conditions become difficult and hard, one is unhappy. One's happiness is determined by outside circumstances.

I believe the Universe is friendly. Now, there are hostile people and hostile environments. Stay away from them. But that doesn't mean that life was designed to be unfriendly and hostile. I believe God/Higher Being/Great Spirit/Universe is full of love and conspiring for my benefit.

Since the Universe is friendly, I believe nothing happens *to* me, everything happens *for* me. I have life lessons, growth areas, and wounds that need to be healed. I believe my life conditions are presented for my benefit, to heal, grow, and awaken.

With this belief system, what is "done unto" me? My happiness is determined not by outside life circumstances, but by my internal processing. I ask myself, what is my lesson? Then, I change my judgmental, limited thinking and use the external condition for a springboard for internal growth.

One of my favorite Far Side cartoons depicts two robots in a psychologist's office for marriage therapy. The two robots have many buttons on their steel bodies. The psychologist says, "The problem, as I see it, is that you both are extremely adept at pushing each other's buttons." The reason most of us can relate to this is because our buttons have been pushed by other people. But if we did not have the buttons, no one could push them.

Here's another way to look at this truth. If you squeeze an orange, you know orange juice will come out. That is what is inside the orange. If someone "squeezes "you, what comes out? Anger? Hostility? Or, an acceptance that allows you to communicate effectively. The person who is hitting your button is showing you what is inside of you. Please look at that interaction has happening *for* you, so you can heal the anger and hostility.

The Universe is friendly and wants us to grow and heal our "buttons." Because of this, people, events, and experiences, show up to shine the light on the healthy and unhealthy aspects of our self. For example, you and I meet a 40-year-old businessman. I leave the meeting and say, "He was kind of an ass." You say, "I thought he was a good guy." Same person. Same experience. Different interpretations. How does that happen?

I might have a negative history of 40-year-old men who dress, talk, and present themselves in the way he did. I look at him through those lenses and project my old negative thoughts, beliefs, and experiences onto him. You might have a positive history of 40-year-old men who show up like he did. You look at him through those lenses and project your positive thoughts, beliefs, and experiences onto him

Who's right? We both are ... for ourselves. It is "done unto" us as we believe.

Author Martha Beck wrote, "People who do destructive things to us are sent to help us find where our belief systems are doing negative things to us already." A person who was raised in an environment where destructive things were told, modeled, and done to her will have emotional wounds. She will tend to stay in situations where people are destructive to her because that is her belief system about herself.

As an adult, this is not happening *to* her, it is happening *for* her. These life experiences are showing her where she needs to reconcile and change the old, destructive belief systems that she was taught. The Universe is showing her an old "button" that needs love, support, and healing.

The good news is that we will no longer be held hostage by the external circumstances of our lives. We have the power to take the inner journey of owning our "buttons" and resolving old issues that are holding us back from living life with meaning and purpose. Jesus said in the Gnostic Gospel of Thomas, verse 70: "If you bring forth what is within you, what you bring forth will save you. If you do not bring forth what is within you, what you do not bring forth will destroy you."

If you have old, destructive beliefs about yourself and life within you, bring them to the light. Talk about them with a trusted person or professional. These old damaging beliefs will lose power and you will be "saved." The result will be a healthier, happier life. If you don't bring them to the light, they will forever reside and guide you to unhealthy and unhappy life situations. "It is done unto you as you believe."

Truth #1: *Your thoughts create your reality.* Deborah thought she needed to fix her alcoholic dad and then needed to fix her husband. That created a reality of tension, chaos, and a lose-lose outcome. Later, Deborah attended Al-Anon and Adult Children of Alcoholic meetings. She learned that she could not change another person. She could only change herself. Slowly, she changed her thoughts about trying to change her husband. Since he did not change his alcoholic behaviors, Deborah changed her reality and left him for a life that included much more peace.

Truth #2: *There is no reality outside your interpretation of it.* Eddie interpreted his life by what was modeled to him by his parents. Eddie's high school teachers saw great potential in Eddie and suggested community college and then a four-year university. Eddie did not interpret his life that way and stayed in the lane his parents prescribed.

Truth #3: *You are not your thoughts.* A person has unproductive thoughts about himself because he was told those things during his childhood. When he's an adult, people show up and say unproductive things to him. Through counseling, he realizes these people are showing him what he already believes about himself. He realizes he is not a bad person. He changes his old belief systems and further realizes he is a person who can flourish and accomplish many productive things.

"It is done unto you as you believe." I hope you *believe* you can have more experiences of happiness than unhappiness. I hope you *believe* you can have more experiences of validation that rejection. I hope you *believe* you can have more experiences of contentment than suffering. Heal the past. Forgive those who have harmed you. Grow toward the light. The Universe is rooting for you.

Reflections

1. Practice seeing life as friendly. Practice seeing life circumstances are *for* you. What are the life lessons that will help propel you to a happier life?
2. What is an example of something that is "done unto you" that is unhealthy and unproductive? Name the belief system that is creating that? Change that belief.
3. Take a calculated risk. Create time with a trusted friend or a professional where you can "bring forth what is within you" so you can learn, heal, and grow.

Chapter 11

K

"Our life always expresses the result of our dominant thoughts."

*Soren **K**ierkegaard*

Kierkegaard was a Danish theologian, poet, author, and is widely accepted as the first existential philosopher. He wrote that life includes much suffering and he had a deep and abiding faith in a mystical God.

The message of this quote grabbed me. I was surprised by how it took hold of me. I asked myself 'why did this one capture me more than the others?' The answer came. I am very conscious of my fleeting thoughts in the present moment. I am good at being aware when a judgmental thought crosses my mind. I see it, and let go of it. I am good at being aware when I have a thought that is resisting life—what is happening in the present moment. I see it and practice letting go of it.

Kierkegaard is talking about dominant thoughts, not the 1,000 fleeting thoughts we have every day. I quickly became aware that I was not fully conscious of my underlying, prevailing dominant thoughts. Because they are foundational, these thoughts govern the rest of my thoughts. Since they will express themselves in my life, I think it's critical that I name them. I found naming my dominant thoughts to be a difficult process. I could easily name my to do list, my thoughts about today's weather, and my frustrating thoughts about trying to name the dominant thoughts and central belief systems.

My first attempt was not honest. I wasn't trying to be deceitful, but the thoughts I listed were mostly thoughts I aspire to. For example, I listed "Be love." I looked at my life, and I am not fully living that thought. That thought is not dominant.

I then switched things around. I looked at what I *express i*n my life. I looked at my dominant behaviors, worked my way back to the thoughts that created those behaviors. I then had my list.

I created another list. I named that one, "Dominant Thoughts I Want To Adopt More Fully." "Be love," was on that list. The most interesting thing has happened since then. I am being more loving. The *result* of naming that *dominant thought* is that I am *expressing* it more often. Thank you, Soren Kierkegaard.

It wasn't an easy exercise, but it was eye-opening. How about you? If you chose to not focus on your minute-by-minute thoughts but rather name the thoughts that dominate your life, could you do that? Try it. Does that list look like the life you want to lead? If it doesn't, do you know you have the power to change it?

I have been sharing this quote with most of my clients. I share with them that the message of the quote has been helping me, and that I think it could help them. The results have been therapeutically amazing.

Jake was a 42-year-old who came into counseling because he said he said he was tired of feeling sad. When I shared Kierkegaard's quote, his eyes welled up with tears. "I don't want to share my dominant thought." I gave him a questioning look. He dabbed his eyes and then said, "Here's my dominant thought: I just want to make it through each day." The tears stayed in his eyes. "I don't want that to be my dominant thought," he said right before he blew his nose.

Jake had been raised in an emotionally abusive home. Jake's mom was divorced and definitely saw every glass as half empty. She allowed abusive men into the family's life and was perpetually negative toward life. Jake was the oldest and had to defend his younger siblings and took the brunt of the abuse.

As an adult, Jake was smart and hard-working, so he was successful in paying the bills and holding a job. But his dominant thought of surviving and merely making it through each and every day was exhausting. During the next couple of sessions, we spent time on crafting a more functional and beneficial dominant thought. At the start of a session, Jake smiled and took a piece of paper out of his wallet.

"I've got a new dominant thought. Here it is."

He read from the folded sheet. "I like life and I trust that with my hard work everything will work out."

"How does that dominant thought feel?" I asked.

"Fantastic," Jake replied. "And the darndest thing, it has been expressing itself in my life." He sat back in the chair. "I now have more energy, I'm a happier husband and father, and I want to take on more at work."

Korrie was raised in an alcoholic home. She was smart and hard-working and had learned co-dependent behaviors. She married Nick, a handsome, charismatic, narcissistic man. He had multiple affairs and a hard time maintaining a job. She had great hopes of changing him during her 20s and early 30s. They had two children and she finally divorced him after 12 years of marriage. She was now dating a good guy and was successful at her job. But she was not happy and always exhausted.

I shared Kierkegaard's quote, and I appropriately disclosed some of my own dominant thoughts about work and family. She thought for a moment, and then said, "My dominant thought about marriage is I don't want to repeat

Nick. I'm so scared of finding another narcissist or drunk, my dominant thought circles around the fear of creating that again." She waited another second or two. "My dominant thought about work is 'Don't fail.'" She hung her head. "Those are two terrible dominant thoughts!"

I asked her why she thought they were terrible.

"Because they are not positive and they are both hanging onto negativity. I will never move forward in life if I'm only thinking about not repeating a Nick relationship and not failing at work."

"What would you like your dominant thoughts to be?"

"I don't know. But I want to create a successful long-term relationship with the guy I'm dating. And I want to thrive at work, not just survive."

"Do you think you just named two new dominant thoughts?"

She smiled. "Yes. I want to try on these thoughts this week and talk next week about whether they were a good fit."

I believe all humans are seeking happiness, yet from unhealthy and dysfunctional thinking, many people are doing things that create suffering. Buddha said this occurs because of ignorance of how thoughts create reality. The antidote to this ignorance is being aware of your dominant thoughts. There is a direct line from these thoughts to emotional states and behaviors in the external world.

Truth #1: *Your thoughts create your reality.* Jake's dominant thought of, "I just want to make it through each day," created a reality of exhaustion and seeing everything as a threat. Korrie's dominant thought of "I don't want to repeat Nick," created a reality of fear and stuck relationships. When they changed their dominant thoughts, their realities changed and they were happier.

Truth #2: *There is no reality outside your interpretation of it.* Without the help of Kierkegaard and counseling, Jake and Korrie would have continued their approaches life because that is the only reality they knew. With awareness, they interpreted life differently and made new realities for themselves.

Truth #3: *You are not your thoughts.* During their childhoods, Jake and Korrie learned to think about their worlds in a certain way. They were not their thoughts of fear and scarcity. Their thoughts created those ways of being in the world. When they created healthier thoughts, they lived in the world in a different way.

Reflections

1. Look at your dominant behaviors. Work yourself back and find the thoughts that create those behaviors. Make a list of your dominant thoughts.
2. What do you think of that list? Do you want to expand your dominant thoughts? Make a new list titled, "Dominant Thoughts I Want To Adopt More Fully."
3. As I was sharing this quote with peers, acquaintances, and friends, a common dominant thought they shared was, "If I get through my workday, then I can be happy." Marcus Buckingham said only 17 percent of the workforce feels fulfilled at work. Are you part of that 17 percent or 83 percent? Do you need to change a dominant thought so you can find fulfillment at work? Or do you need to change jobs?

Chapter 12

L

"All our knowledge has its origins in our perceptions."

Leonardo da Vinci

Leonardo da Vinci was an Italian Renaissance Man. He is widely considered one of the greatest painters of all time. His areas of interest also included invention, sculpture, architecture, science, philosophy, and engineering.

There is a Hindu and Buddhist parable about six blind men who lived in the same village. One day the villagers told them there was an elephant in the village. They had no idea what an elephant was so they decided that since they could not see the elephant, they would each go and feel it with their hands. They went to the village and each put their hands on the elephant.

The first man touched his leg. He, said, "The elephant is like a pillar."

The second man touched the tail. "Oh no, it is like a rope."

The third man touched the trunk of the elephant. "No, no. It is like a thick branch of a tree."

The fourth man felt the ear. "You're all wrong. It is like a big hand fan."

The fifth man touched the belly. "It is like a wall."

Finally, the sixth man touched the tusk. "It is like a solid pipe."

They argued about the nature of the elephant. Each man insisted that he was right. The situation was escalating when a wise man passed by them. He stopped and asked them about their argument. "We cannot agree what the elephant is like," one of the men said. Each one shared what he thought the elephant was like. The wise man calmly explained, "All of you are right. The reason every one of you is telling it differently is because each of you touched a different part of the elephant. Actually, the elephant has all those features each of you described."

The anger of each of the six men dissipated. They no longer had a need to argue.
The moral of the story is everyone has their own perception. There may be truth to what each person shares. Sometimes we agree with another person's "truth," and sometimes, because he or she may have different perceptions which we disagree, we argue like the blind men.

It is always fair to state your perception—your "truth"—with open ears and no attachment to altering the other person's view. When you argue and try to change another person, this usually causes the other person to dig further into their "truth." Instead, listen and be tolerant. We can live in harmony and have different perceptions of reality.

To perceive means to become aware through the five senses. Since all we know we have either heard, seen, touched, smelled, or felt, our knowledge is an aggregate of all our perceptions. Gaining this knowledge began in our childhood. We learned "truth" through the perceptions our family members had toward life. If their perceptions were skewed toward the unhealthy, we have a tendency to adopt those perceptions. For example, if your parents had negative perceptions toward people in power like bosses or politicians, you have likely adopted those perceptions. You "know" that those people are corrupt and self-serving. As an adult, you might investigate those familial perceptions, and conclude they are not correct.

Everything is perception. We think we are observing an objective reality, but it is solely a subjective reality. Everything is filtered through our thoughts, beliefs, assumptions, preconceptions, and experiences. It has been said that we do not see things as they are, but as *we* are.

Now let's return to Leonardo's quote, "All our knowledge has its origins in our perceptions." What is your "knowledge" about family? Have you learned through your five senses that family is a loving place where everyone has each other's backs? Or have you learned that family is a place where you have to protect yourself from others who are abusive? What is your "knowledge" about others? Have you learned that most people are good and its emotionally safe to be vulnerable and ask for help when needed? Or have you learned that the world is not a safe place and it's an "eat or be eaten" world?

What is your "knowledge" about work? Is work a four letter word and is it something to be endured? Or have your learned that work is a place to share your talents and gifts? What is your "knowledge" about money? Is it a scare commodity and the biggest emotional battle within your marriage? Or have you learned that money is simply numbers? You and your life partner talk about the numbers that come in and decide how to "spend" the numbers.

Heidi came into counseling because her 30-year-old single daughter was emotionally abusive to her. Heidi grew up in a home where she was the caregiver to her divorced mother. Her mom played the role of the victim and made Heidi cook, clean, and play the mother role to her younger sister. Heidi's "knowledge" of family was you needed to give, give, and then give some more. She did that for her only child, who never married, and worked sporadically. Heidi asked in a counseling session if her daughter's adult behaviors were normal. I answered her question with another question. "Do you want to keep paying your daughter's expenses and taking her abuse?"

"No," she quickly answered.

"You can't change your daughter but you can change yourself," I reflected to her. "You never learned how to set boundaries in your childhood. Now you're ready to learn how to say 'no' and set healthy boundaries." Heidi slowly and incrementally set boundaries with her daughter. They talked less on the phone, but Heidi was okay with that.

Truth #1: *Your thoughts create your reality.* Heidi was taught it was her job to take care of all family members. That thought pattern led her to maintain a parent-child relationship with her adult daughter. Heidi changed her thoughts which created an adult-adult reality with her adult daughter.

Truth #2: *There is no reality outside your interpretation of it.* Heidi's interpretation of family was harming her. A good question to ask yourself is, "Where are you getting harmed?" Your interpretation of money? Friends? Family? Work? Change your interpretation and practice living a new way.

Truth #3: *You are not your thoughts.* Heidi is not her thoughts—either healthy or unhealthy— about her family. You are not your thoughts about any dynamic in your life. You have the freedom to change your thoughts.

Leonardo da Vinci also said, "Iron rusts from disuse; water loses its purity from stagnation ... even so does inaction sap the vigor of the mind." If you have not actively looked at your life and considered changing perceptions of areas where you are stuck and unhappy, you are "rusting" from disuse of your powerful mind. Make your mind a wonderful servant and check out your old perceptions with trusted friends, or read books, or talk with a professional counselor. This feedback can help you create new perceptions which will help move you forward.

Reflections

1. A person you know is happier at work than you. You now realize you might be looking at only one aspect of the "elephant" (work). Ask them to share their view of work.
2. Is there a quote or a scripture that you think is too Pollyanna-ish or unobtainable? Create a meeting with your minister or a trusted friend and ask him/her about his/her perception of that quote.
3. It's Monday and your "knowledge" about Mondays is like the Mamas and Papas' song of the 1960s: "You can't trust that day." Change your perception about Monday and create the thought that it will include happiness and joy.

Chapter 13

M

"If you don't like something, change it. If you can't change it, change your attitude."

Maya Angelou

Angelou was an American poet, memoirist, and civil rights activist. In 1993, she recited her poem, *On the Pulse of the Morning*, at Bill Clinton's inauguration.

This quote has two parts and both are equally powerful and challenging. The first, "If you don't like something, change it," challenges us to be change agents. The opposite of this is a victim or a complainer. These roles keep us stuck and create negativity.

A change agent is a person who sees that something is not working and does something about it. She sees an old thought pattern that is creating negativity in her life, so she practices changing her thoughts. He sees an injustice in the world and tries to bring justice. She sees a better way to do something and starts working on doing it. Sometimes it takes more than one person to create the change, so others are motivated to be part of the change.

Many, many people want to take the path of least resistance and are not change agents. They would rather sit in the break room and complain about their work or politics. They would rather be unhappy than attempt to make something better. These people are probably not reading this book.

You are reading this book. You are open to change. You are open to making your community better. You are open to making the world better. You are open to making yourself better.

How could you more fully be a change agent? Is there a dynamic in your marriage or a friendship that calls you to communicate and ask for what you need? Is there an international or national issue, like climate change, poverty, or access to clean water, where you can make your own incremental change?

The parable below, adopted from *The Star Thrower*, by Loren Eiseley, shows us that we can make a difference when we become change agents:

An old man was walking along the shore after a big storm had passed through. The beach was littered with starfish. The old man noticed a young boy approaching. The young lad would lean over, pick up a starfish, and throw it back into the ocean. The old man asked the boy what he was doing. "The storm and tide washed these starfish up onto the beach. They can't return to the sea by themselves, so I'm throwing them back into the water." The old man replied, "There are hundreds and hundreds of starfish on the beach. I'm afraid you won't really be able to make a difference." The boy bent down, picked up a starfish and threw it back into the ocean. "I made a difference to that one."

The second line of Angelou's quote, "If you can't change it, change your attitude," challenges us to be aware of our thoughts and, when necessary, be flexible and adopt new thoughts. This reminds me of a favorite joke, "How many psychologists does it take to change a light bulb? One, but the light bulb has to want to change." I've told this joke to many clients when they are unsuccessfully trying to change another person. The humor helps loosen the client's emotional grip on the person he is trying to change.

I share with these clients that I, as a professional counselor, cannot change anyone. I can create an environment where change can occur. But I can't change anyone. In my office, I share an Al-Anon strategy that helps a person to let go and not try to control another person. The tactic is to ask yourself the question, "Is my name in that sentence?" If your name is in the sentence, that means they are asking you for advice and so you may share.

The clients usually nod their heads because it makes sense. Then we work on the strategies of how to emotionally let go and let it be. For example, there is a person in your life you think has an alcohol problem. Or, you think a person is dating someone who is not good for that person. Or, a person is taking a job that you think is not a good fit and will not earn enough money. In the three examples above, they are not asking for your opinion— your name is not in that sentence—so you can let go and wish them well.

Do you notice a difference in these two sentences: "I really like Betty and I'm glad she's in my life." "I really like Betty. Pete, do you think we're a good fit?"
My name is not in the first sentence, so I would politely respond that I am glad he likes Betty. My name *is* in the second sentence and I can give respectful feedback.

Frank and Phyllis came into my office because their only child, a 30-year-old son and his wife, had said that they had decided to not have children. They said that they loved their son and daughter-in-law no matter what, but what was making them sad was the realization they would never have grandchildren. Their sadness was getting in the way of a living a full and happy life.

Phyllis and Frank were in the midst of the grieving process. They saw the joy their friends were experiencing with their grandchildren. They were sad that this would not be part of their lives. They were no longer in the denial or bargaining stages of grief. They said that they had never been angry. They were in the sad stage and couldn't move past it.

The last stage of grief is acceptance. Acceptance occurs when you change your attitude about something you cannot change. Acceptance does not mean it is wonderful that grandchildren are not part of your future, but you are going to be okay with a life of without them. I told Frank and Phyllis that I would help them through their grieving process, and they would come to terms with their new reality. I also shared with them that there would be good days and not-so-good days, and with acceptance, they would move on with their lives and get involved in normal activities again.

They could not change their son and daughter-in-law. So they slowly, incrementally changed their attitude. Frank and Phyllis led a happier life.

Truth #1: *Your thoughts create your reality.* Frank and Phyllis had a thought that created a reality of sadness that was moving toward depression. They changed their thoughts, started working through the stages of grief, and their new reality was closer to their old lives which included church activities, a bridge group that entered tournaments, and a big garden in their backyard.

Truth #2: *There is no reality outside your interpretation of it.* Frank and Phyllis interpreted the reality of no grandchildren as depressing. Their son interpreted it as no big deal. A same-sex couple might interpret it as an obstacle and work on options which would result in having a child. These are different interpretations of the same reality.

Truth #3: *You are not your thoughts.* Frank and Phyllis did not realize that their attitude about not having grandchildren was creating their emotional states. Once they realized they could accept this new reality, they changed their *attitudes*—their thoughts—which allowed them to re-claim their lives.

William James was an American philosopher and psychologist and the first educator to offer a psychology course in the United States. He said, "The greatest discovery of our generation is that human beings can alter their lives by altering their attitudes of mind. As you think, so shall you be." If you don't change your attitude about situations that you cannot change, you will suffer. That means the other person is not creating your suffering, you are. Take responsibility, let go, change your attitude, and live a happy, productive life.

Reflections

1. Name something you have been contemplating changing in your life. Make a plan this week to implement that change.
2. Name something or someone you have been trying to change. You now realize you do not have the power to change them. Name your change in attitude. How does that feel?
3. Is there a grief issue in your life where you have not reached the stage of acceptance? Name a "change of attitude" that will allow you to accept that grief issue.

Chapter 14

N

"What the mind of man can conceive and believe, it can achieve."

Napoleon Hill

Napoleon Hill was a 20th century self-help author. He is known best for his book *Think and Grow Rich,* which is the fifth best-selling self-help book of all time. His work revolved around the role of personal beliefs in the success of an individual. He is widely credited to have influenced many people into success.

As stated in the Introduction, there is a progression to how we operate in our internal and external worlds. Everything starts in the internal world of our mind which creates our thoughts. Our thoughts create our feelings which then lead to the behaviors we make in the external world. Napoleon Hill's research has boiled down how our lives operate to a simple formula. The thoughts that we *conceive* or create in our mind, plus your *belief* that it's true for you, equals the ability to *achieve* it in your lives.

This is a very powerful belief. Hill is saying we can achieve what we put our mind to. You can create very productive, healthy, and widespread fruitful outcomes. You can also create hurtful, unhealthy, unproductive outcomes with widespread detrimental effects. As Peter Parker's Uncle Ben says in *Spiderman*, "With great power comes great responsibility."

This scope of this power is on a continuum. You can conceive and believe incredibly healthy and productive thoughts and find great meaning and purpose in life. The opposite is also true: you can create a life where you feel stuck and depressed. You can also conceive and believe both healthy and unhealthy thoughts, which puts you in the middle of the continuum. Most people say balance is important, but not in this case. With this mentality, you are close to the unhealthy side of having unproductive and toxic thoughts about yourself and your life. These unhealthy thoughts you *conceive and believe* keep you limited, stuck, and unhappy in life to the degree of your place on the continuum.

Let's put a couple of truths together. First, everything starts with a thought. Second, your thoughts create your reality. Third, what goes around, comes around. If your thoughts are angry and judgmental, your reality will be agitated and non-peaceful. If you are putting out anger, judgment, and agitation into your world, you get that back. Then a self-fulfilling prophecy occurs. You are receiving this negativity which reinforces your negative thinking. You are stuck. You are responsible for what you create.

The word *responsible* has two words in it; able and response. This means you are *able* to *respond* to any situation. With this ability, choose to respond to the world in a new way. Change your thoughts to accepting what is occurring. This will give you freedom to be more flexible and adaptable. You will be more peaceful and then you will receive that back from others. A new self-fulfilling prophecy will occur. You will expect the world to be friendly and helpful.

If you are conscious of experiencing an unfriendly environment—which you created—it is the necessary first step toward creating peace. The hostility or unpleasantness is the message to change your thoughts about the situation. In fact, the opposite of that painful thought will move you toward contentment. Have your mind *conceive* more functional thoughts. Then *believe* these thoughts will be healthier for you and the others around you. Then *achieve* those ideas. If you have to, fake it until you make it. Quit resisting what is. It has happened. You are *able* to *respond* in a more peaceful and functional manner. Maybe it's leaving the situation or communicating in a more effective manner. You are the creator of your world.

Audrey was a 20-year-old college student who came to my office with symptoms of depression. She had a 3.95 GPA, was active in her sorority, and was a Pre-Med major. Both parents were medical doctors. They told Audrey since 9th grade to take classes that would prepare her for her Pre-Med major. She was told that competition is fierce for medical school, so she needed to start early to have the best application.

During one of our sessions, Audrey said she did not want to apply to medical school. She wanted to switch majors and become a teacher. Through her tears, she said she couldn't tell her parents this and she was stuck in a major she didn't like and a future profession that wasn't a good fit for her.

Audrey had not *conceived* or *believed* any of her own thoughts about her college major or career. She adopted the thoughts her parents conceived and believed about her. Sadly, this created Audrey's depression. If Audrey were allowed the freedom to choose her own thoughts about school and work, she would *conceive* the thoughts of being an elementary school teacher. She *believed* she would be a good teacher. These thoughts made Audrey feel happy.

In time, Audrey took the risk and communicated to her parents about her desire to change majors. Her parents slowly let go of their expectations. Audrey changed her major, the depression lifted, and she achieved her goal of becoming a teacher.

Truth #1: *Your thoughts create your reality.* Audrey's thoughts of chemistry, biology, anatomy, and other Pre-Med classes made her depressed. Her reality lightened when she changed her thoughts, communicated to her parents, and changed her major.

Truth #2: *There is no reality outside your interpretation of it.* Medical school has no meaning. It is, in and of itself, value neutral. Audrey's parents created their own interpretation of it. They thought it was noble and brought high esteem. Audrey had her own interpretation. She saw medical school as uninteresting and arduous. Two different realities about the same entity.

Truth #3: *You are not your thoughts.* Both Audrey and her parents changed their thoughts about medical school for her. They were the same people they had been before and after they changed their thoughts. The thoughts were the only things that changed.

Most people follow what they have been taught and modeled. If your parents *conceived, believed* and *achieved* limiting goals of "color within the lines," "make just enough money to pay the bills," and "keep your head down," you are prone to *conceive, believe* and *achieve* similar goals.

This quote from Napoleon Hill says you can achieve what you put your mind to. What is stopping you from living a bigger life that has positive ripple effects to many, many people? Author Marianne Williamson wrote, "Our deepest fear is not that we are inadequate. Our deepest fear is that we are powerful beyond measure." Ask yourself if you are fearful of doing something different than your peers and family? What would happen if you followed an inner dream of creating a graphic novel? Mentor a youth who is at risk for unhealthy behaviors? Create an environmental movement at your workplace? Change careers?

If you have fearful thoughts of failing, I hope you let them go and create other, more functional thoughts that allow you to take a calculated risk. If you have fears of living to your potential, I hope you change those thoughts about that, too. You are here to do magnificent things. You are here to change your world. You are here to live a life of making wide-ranging positive impacts. Believe it! Think bigger. Aim higher. What your mind can conceive and believe, it can achieve. You are powerful beyond measure.

Reflections
1. Write one, two, or three things you want to achieve. Start the conscious practice of conceiving and believing those ideas.
2. Be responsible! Figure out where in your life you are *able* to *respond* differently.
3. Where in your life do you want to be "powerful beyond measure?" Take calculated risks to start that process.

Chapter 15

O

"Whatever follows your 'I am' will always come looking for you."

*Joel **O**steen*

Osteen is a pastor and author of ten books. His church services are seen in over 100 countries.

Your sense of identity is formed by your thoughts. For example, *I am* too fat or skinny are thoughts. *I am* athletic or a computer geek, are thoughts. *I am* a sinful person or child of God are thoughts.

You can change your thoughts about yourself. For example, "I don't like my body weight and *I am* disciplined so *I am* going to eat healthier and work out." Or, "*I am* athletic but I want marketable job skills so *I am* going to become more computer literate."

Did you notice all the *I am* statements in the two previous paragraphs? Remember, "Whatever follows your 'I am' will always come looking for you." *I am* fat means not changing eating habits and being fat will always come looking for you because that is how you identify yourself. *I am* disciplined means you will stick to a regimen because that is how you perceive who you are. *I am* going to eat healthier will come looking for you and you will purchase healthier foods. You will take computer classes because you told yourself *I am* going to become more computer literate.

Osteen's quote is powerful because your sense of self—your identity—drives how you will live in the world.

Your thoughts create your identity. *I am* is a thought. It is up to you how you want to live in the world.

Mark was a new client. When I asked him in the first session what he wanted to talk about he said, "I am an emotional eater." I asked Mark what he did after he said that to himself. He said, "I go to the grocery store and buy a bag of Reese's peanut butter cups and eat the whole bag."

I knew the power of *I am* statements so I taught this truth to Mark. Then, I asked him what new "I am" statements he would like to make. He didn't have to think very long before he said, "I am strong. I am healthy. I am happy."

Next week when Mark came into my office, the first thing he said was, "Pete, those 'I am' statements really work. I didn't go to the store to buy candy once this week!" It has ebbed and flowed since then, because sometimes Mark would unconsciously go back to previous "I am" statements. But Mark became more conscious of his thoughts and even if, out of habit, he wanted to buy Reese's peanut butter cups, he would say to himself, *I am strong, I am healthy, I am happy.* Strong, healthy, and happy came looking for him.

Jessica is 55-year-old and a university professor of education. She loves to teach literacy and help education students become outstanding teachers. For 25 years, one of her "I am" statements is "I am a teacher of education."

The university in which Jessica works wants her to teach more from the textbook that their local public school system uses. That way the students will be better prepared to teach that text book material once they secure a local job.

Jessica's love is to teach social justice, help marginalized children, and build relationships. She wants to teach her students critical thinking skills, how to integrate teaching with larger issues, along with teaching the nuts and bolts of how to be a successful teacher.

Jessica has been unhappy for a couple of years because the administration gives her lower marks on her annual performance review because she is not solely teaching from the textbook. She came into my office in a level of existential crisis.

I heard Jessica's statement of "I am a teacher of education," and I heard her say that the current administration is not allowing her to teach in a way that she thinks is important. Her *I am* statement is being stymied. Jessica needed to grieve the loss of being the professor she wanted to be.

During the next counseling session, I heard Jessica say she would enjoy working for the Children's Defense Fund and help advocate for social justice and marginalized children. I asked Jessica if she had an "I am" statement within that vision. She thought for a minute and said, "I am a person who helps decide national policy on these issues."

I asked her, "How does that make you feel?"

She smiled and said "good." She looked like she was thinking so I waited.

She then said, "I will finish this academic year, and I will look for a job in the meantime."

I believe in Jessica and I believe in the power of *I am* statements. I believe a national or local position of education/advocacy/policy making will *come looking for* her.

Truth #1: *Your thoughts create your reality.* Mark's thought of "I am an emotional eater," created a reality of eating unhealthy foods and gaining weight. Jessica's thought of "I am a teacher," got her into a teaching job at a university. When Mark changed his thoughts about eating, and the university's structure created the opportunity for

Jessica to change her thoughts, healthier realities were created for both of them.

Truth #2: *There is no reality outside your interpretation of it.* Mark thought his reality was being an emotional eater. He changed his reality by changing his *I am* statements. Jessica thought her reality was being a cutting edge university professor. Her reality was full of frustration because of a university policy. She changed that reality by changing her *I am* statement to one that would fit her better.

Truth #3: *You are not your thoughts.* "I am an emotional eater" are merely words that come from a thought. That is not Mark. That is what Mark did when he experienced emotional turmoil.

Reinhold Niebuhr was an American theologian, author, and professor at Union Theological Seminary for over 30 years. He received the Presidential Medal of Freedom in 1964. His book *The Nature and Destiny of Man* is ranked 18th of the top 100 non-fiction books of the 20th century. He said, "Change is the essence of life; be willing to surrender what you are for what you could become."

Your *I am* statements change throughout your lifetime, based on how well you are handling a life issue. Be open to change when a previous *I am* statement has run its course and you are in need to "surrender" that for "what you could become."

This is exciting. You have complete control. Make a commitment to thrive and manifest the wonderful gifts and talents you have inside of you.

Reflections

1. Name some of your *I am* statements. What do you think of them? Any you want to let go of? Any you want to tweak a little bit? Any new ones you want to add?

2. Here are two different practices: a) You physically feel a little off. Say to yourself, "I am healthy. I am healthy. I am healthy." b) You are going to ask for a raise. Say to yourself, "I am worthy. I am worthy. I am worthy."

3. Research shows that our identity changes throughout our lifetime. Have you gone through a developmental or life change yet kept an old identity? Do you need to create new *I am* statement in any section of your life?

Chapter 16

P

*"Let any man examine his thoughts and he will
find them ever occupied with the past and the
future. We scarcely think at all of the present."*

*Blaise **Pascal***

Pascal was a 17th century French philosopher, theologian,
and scientist and one of
the greatest and most influential mathematicians of all time.

Generally, people who think in the past are more
prone to being depressed. They can be stuck in the past
with perceived positive or negative life events. For
example, a 45-year-old man might have depressing
thoughts because he is no longer living the glory days of
his high school football successes. Or, a woman might have
depressing thoughts because she is still thinking about her
ex-husband who cheated on her 10 years ago.

Generally, people who think in the future are more
prone to being anxious. Their thoughts are usually about
negative outcomes that could happen. For example, a
parent might think, "What if my 18-year-old child gets into
an accident tonight on his date?" An employee might think,
"What happens if my job gets deported? What if the
economy goes into another major recession?" These are all
thoughts of fear. The four letters of fear could represent,
Future Events Appearing Real. This is the recipe for
anxiety.

The only things that are real are in the present moment. The past is an illusion. It is gone. The future is an illusion. It has yet to appear.

Remember how we operate? Everything starts with a thought.

Thoughts create feelings, which coupled together lead to our behaviors. The thoughts and associated feelings about the future may feel real. But they are coming from fabricated thoughts that are not based on fact or reality. The anxious feelings are generated from the thoughts we make up about the future.

"The mind is a wonderful servant, but a terrible master." This powerful proverb can help us re-claim power in our life. From reading the previous chapters and with practice, you are seeing that you are not your thoughts. You have the power to stop your mind from pushing you to the past or the future. You have the power to consciously use your mind—not to be controlled by it.

A good strategy to make your mind a "wonderful servant" is to write about the thoughts that tend to be "masters" over you. This creates distance and will allow you to see the abusive power these thoughts have. Then write new thoughts that are grounded in the present moment. The result will be peace and freedom.

Another good strategy is to realize that feelings are messengers. For example, if you are feeling anxious, ask yourself, "What is the message from that feeling?" The message is probably to see that your thoughts are creating "what if" outcomes in the future, and you need to re-focus your mind to the present moment.

My mind tends to drift to the past or the future when I'm driving. I'll be driving to work and suddenly I feel anxious about some matter. I know that feelings are messengers, so I honor the message to let go of the future-oriented thoughts and come back to the present moment. To do that, I feel my butt in the seat. I feel my hands on the steering wheel. I might crack the window to feel the wind against my face. All these strategies ground me in the present moment.

It is important and necessary to look to the future to plan and set goals. But once you are done looking to see where you want to go, then you need to come back to the present moment and implement those plans. This is an example of you controlling your thoughts, instead of your thoughts controlling you.

Ted was a doctoral student who was writing his dissertation. He came into my office because of intense anxiety. Ted said that he couldn't sleep at night because his mind would race. He felt paralyzed and could not finish his dissertation because he worried that it was not good enough.

Ted said things like, "What if the professors say my dissertation is a piece of shit?" "What happens if my research numbers don't match the hypothesis?" "What will I do for a livelihood if I don't get my PhD?"

I reflected to Ted that all of his questions—his thoughts—were future-oriented. He agreed and defended those thoughts by saying that he needed to look in that direction. I asked him how he felt when his thoughts were directed to the future? He answered "terrible," but still defended his way of thinking.

I asked Ted what he needed to do *today* for his dissertation. He rattled off a few things. I then asked Ted how he felt when he thought about accomplishing that list. He said good. I then asked Ted after he completed *today's* projects, would he then create a things-to-do list for tomorrow. He thought for a moment and said he would. I asked him how that made him feel. He said good.

Ted was not connecting the dots to see that by working on his dissertation in the present moment, it would lead to positive feelings and relieve his feelings of anxiety.

So I helped Ted come to that insight. He still defended his habit of thinking about the future. I used a therapy technique and said, "Ted, you may continue to think that way if you want to have anxiety rule your life."

My honesty startled him. He sat back in his chair and thought about it. Then he smiled. "Okay," he said. "I will practice, every day, making a things-to-do list and keeping my mind directed only on that."

Truth #1: *Your thoughts create your reality.* Ted's reality was full of anxiety. His thoughts created that. With insight and practice, he changed his thoughts, which changed his feelings, which changed his behaviors. He crossed the dissertation finish line with fewer feelings of anxiety.

Truth #2: *There is no reality outside your interpretation of it.* Initially, Ted was sure he would fail with his doctoral dissertation. With help, Ted changed his thinking to focus on the present moment, and then he saw the dissertation as something he could accomplish.

Truth #3: *You are not your thoughts.* It is lucky for all of us that this is true. Specifically, Ted is grateful that he is not destined to be anxious the rest of his life. He changed his thoughts, slept better, and completed his dissertation.

My wife and I have two dogs. We see them have stressful moments, and then they shake their whole body which brings them back to the present moment. Their tails wag, and they are back to loving us unconditionally. They are back to reality: the present moment.

Henry David Thoreau wrote, "You must live in the present, launch yourself on every wave, find your eternity in each moment." Don't be like the masses who, according

105

to Blaise Pascal, *scarcely think at all of the present*. Be healthy and productive. Live like a dog. Shake off the past, think and live in the present moment.

Reflections

1. Monitor your thoughts. How often do you find yourself thinking about the past or the future? Gently, seriously, and firmly bring your thoughts back to the present moment.
2. Challenge yourself for a week to journal about how often your mind was a "wonderful servant," and how often it was a "terrible master." Re-read your journal and use it as a tool to make you more aware of your thoughts.
3. Do you agree that the past and the future are illusions? If so, practice letting go of the past hurts and the future anxieties, and think about what is true right now. Do you need to do something today? Then do it. If your mind drifts to the future, write down those thoughts on a things-to-do list. Then come back to the present moment.

Chapter 17

Q

"You cannot get an A if you're afraid of getting an F."

Quincy Jones

Quincy Jones is an American record producer, musician, film producer, and composer. Jones has amassed 80 Grammy Award nominations, 28 Grammys, and a Grammy Legend Award in 1992.

     Jones's quote illustrates two powerful ways to think. One is paradoxical thinking, which allows you to see the whole picture before you make a decision. The other is fear, which is a powerful in an unhealthy way because it's life-draining and an impotent way of thinking and living.

     A paradox is a statement that is seemingly contradictory or opposed to common sense and yet is perhaps true. Paradoxical thinking embraces "both-and" thinking instead of "either-or" thinking. For example, I am both strong and weak. I am both a saint and a sinner. I am both generous and selfish. Paradoxes are two ends of the same continuum. They are interdependent and co-exist with one another. Each depends upon the other for meaning. For example, you cannot understand night without day. You cannot understand the value of an A if there isn't an F.

     Modern culture has a difficult time accepting the "both-and" thinking. People are much more comfortable with the dualistic "either-or" thinking. For example, on election night, all the television stations list states as *either* Red *or* Blue. We know that all the 50 states have a combination of *both* conservatives *and* liberals. Each of the states should be different shades of purple. But for ease and to put everything in an "either-or" box, the television stations report in this too-simple way.

If we are honest, most of our experiences include a mixture of *both* good *and* bad times. For example, beginning an exercise program will be *both* painful *and* pleasurable. By being conscious of both ends of this continuum, you might actually exercise because you know the pain will pass and you will soon feel the pleasure of a body that is in better shape. Everybody has *both* good *and* bad traits. By being aware of these traits, you will be prepared to communicate effectively or more easily let go when a person's negative traits appear.

A "both-and" outlook is open to everything that comes its way. You will be more awake and better able to handle difficult situations. The "either-or" dichotomy discards the parts of reality that you don't like. Then you will be surprised when the difficult comes and you're ill prepared to handle it.

The non-dual consciousness teaches us how to live fully in this dynamic, all-encompassing world that includes *both* the yin *and* the yang, which always includes both dark and light. Paradoxical thinking creates a balance between the opposite ends of the continuum. You will be more likely to find ease living with *both* action *and* contemplation, *both* serving others *and* taking care of yourself, and starting a new project or taking a class where there is a possibility of getting *both* an A *and* an F.

The second part of Quincy Jones's quote refers to fear, which is merely a thought. The reason fear might seem bigger is because it creates powerful feelings. You feel the dread, terror, panic, or worry, and because of their potency, you then think the fear is something real.

Fear differs from danger. Danger is real. The car crossing over the yellow line toward you is real. Do something about it ... quickly. The tiger facing the caveman is real. He needs to quickly escape or he will be eaten.

Fear is the ego mind's way of destroying you. Ego is like a parasite. It will devour its host until the host dies. The good news is you have control over your thoughts. You can "see" your thoughts and if they are unhealthy or unproductive, you can let them go. The parasite will leave the host.

I am an adjunct professor at a local college that primarily serves non-traditional students. At the beginning of each semester, I hear a 35-year-old state, "I haven't been in a classroom for 17 years. I am scared, but I have enrolled because I want to overcome my fear of college classes."

Good for her! She hasn't been in a class for 17 years—that is a fact. Being scared is merely a thought. Overcoming that fear is merely a thought. Which one do you want to manifest? Do you want to stay stuck professionally and never get promoted because you didn't earn a degree? Or do you want to create forward motion to the bigger life that you were meant to live?
She might get an F. She might get an A. How will she know? By taking a calculated risk and leaning into the thought of "I won't know until I try."

T.J. was a senior in high school and the number one seed on his golf team. He was a natural athlete and had a smooth, natural golf swing. He wanted to go to counseling to deal with the issue of falling short of his potential, especially in important golf matches. T.J. was a mature 18-year-old. A parent accompanied T.J. to our first session, but T.J. did all the talking and was clear about what problem he wanted to confront.

"When nothing is on the line, I can drive, chip, and putt the golf ball very well. But when a match is tight or my team needs me to place high, I get tight and tense, and then I don't play as well," T.J. said to me.

"What are the thoughts going through your mind at those times?" I asked him.

He looked down and said softly, "I know this is bad, but I say to myself, 'Don't screw up. Don't screw up.'"

"You're afraid of failing?" I asked him.

T.J. was still looking at the carpet. "Yeah."

Luckily, one of my interests was sports psychology, and I guessed he had read one of the most popular golf psychology books. "T.J., you know the book the Bob Rotella wrote?"

He finally lifted his head., "Yeah. Golf is Not a Game of Perfect. Why?"

"Because—as the title states—golfers constantly fail. Even the pros. Do you want me to give you examples of Tiger Woods failing? Or Rory McIlory?"

He smiled. "No. I know some of their epic failures."

"Okay. You, Tiger, Rory, and every golfer, need to learn how to handle failure because that will allow you to find success."

"I want to find success," he said. "How do I handle failure?"

"First, understand that failure will occur. Accept it. Practice not being fearful of it."

"Accept it?" he asked incredulously.

"Heck yes. What's a professional baseball player who hits .333 make a year?"

"Millions."

"Yes. And he 'fails' 2 out of 3 times at bat. But each time he tries to figure out why he struck out so he won't make the mistake next time."

T.J. chuckled. "Be okay with failure. Learn my lesson. I will then find success."

I smiled back to him. "I wish my adult clients would learn so quickly."

Truth #1: *Your thoughts create your reality.* "Don't fail," was T.J.'s thought. One's mind will now only remember the word 'fail.' It is always best to make a statement in the positive. That is why they are called affirmations. T.J. changed his "Don't fail,' to "I am a competitor." (The *I am* statements discussed in Chapter 15). Later, T.J. reported that he was playing better and more competitive.

Truth #2: *There is no reality outside your interpretation of it.* T.J. interpreted a tight match as tense and nerve-racking. That created a reality of not playing to his potential. T.J. changed his interpretation of a close match to a way to show himself and his team he was a competitor.

Truth #3: *You are not your thoughts.* T.J. is not "Do not screw up." He is also not "I am okay with failure." Those thoughts guide him on how he will play golf. It is vitally important to be conscious of your thoughts because they will always guide you.

One of the great philosophical figures of the 21st century is the *Star* Wars character Yoda. He said, "Fear is the path to the Dark Side. Fear leads to anger, anger leads to hate, hate leads to suffering." By being open and accepting of the paradoxes in your life, you will find compassion which is the greatest antidote to fear. Love your dark side, and then let go of those "F's" in life. With practice, you will soon earn higher grades ... even an "A."

Reflections

1. Spend some time naming some paradoxes of your life. For example, you are *both* a loving parent *and* you can be an angry parent. How comfortable do

you feel with these contradictions? Practice living more on the healthy and productive side.

2. Name a recent "F" experience in your life. Now name the practices that will raise that grade. How does that feel?

3. Most clients come into my office because there is something "bad" in their lives. When they start healing, learning, and growing, I reflect to them one of my favorite paradoxes: You are creating "good" from the "bad." You are fully capable of doing this in your life. If you need help, get help. Live this powerful paradox.

Chapter 18

R

"No one can make you feel inferior without your consent."

*Eleanor **Roosevelt***

Eleanor Roosevelt served as First Lady of the United States. She served as the United States Delegate to the United Nations General Assembly. President Harry Truman later called her "First Lady of the World" in acknowledgment to her human rights achievements.

You have read throughout this book that your thoughts create your reality. Roosevelt's quote is referring to one's self esteem, which is a person's subjective cognitive and emotional evaluation of his or her self. Self-esteem is also formed by your thoughts.

Because there is no reality outside our interpretation of it (Truth #2), self-esteem is subjective. It is connected to how we *perceive* all our characteristics. For example, a person gives a presentation at a work meeting. You thought she did well and you compliment her. She deflected the positive feedback and gave you all the reasons she thought she performed terribly. Two different interpretations of the same reality. The opposite is also true. You thought the presenter missed the mark and later in the day you share that with her. She listens, considers the input, doesn't let the negativity permeate her, and explains why she thought she did a good job.

How you view yourself is a vitally important component of a happy, well-adjusted life. Research shows that low self-esteem increases the likelihood of depression, anxiety, oversensitivity, and loneliness. Lower self-esteem can cause problems with romantic relationships, friendships, and job performance. It can also lead to increased vulnerability to drug and alcohol abuse.

If you have low self-esteem, you probably learned it during your childhood. Maybe your parents reflected more negative than positive things to you. This is called critical parenting. You then have an internal critic that tells you that you are not doing a good enough job. The good news is you can learn a new, healthier way to live in the world. You must now start parenting yourself. In a healthy, positive way, be compassionate and give yourself a break if you mess up. Learn the lesson and tell yourself you will do better next time.

Growth is always an inside job. The inside job is to be aware of your thoughts and not allow the "critical parent" to win. Out of habit, the critical thoughts will appear. Realize that they are merely thoughts, let them go, and then create more functional thoughts.

If you need praise, pats on the back from everybody, encouragement, and constant approval, you are too dependent on others for your self-esteem. This dependency makes you a slave to others, and everybody is your master and judge. This is an environment where you at risk for feeling *inferior.* This is also a starting point to move inward and parent yourself in a healthy way. No one can *make you feel inferior*.

If your life partner never expresses appreciation for your healthy traits, it is fair to ask him or her for more positive feedback. All of us need a nurturing, positive environment. We also need to "parent" ourselves and see the good things we are doing. As you learned in Chapter 15, take time to discern your positive and healthy traits and then make them more conscious by saying "I am" statements during the day. Start with a list of three traits.

You will start seeing more of your positive qualities. Expand your "I am" statements to four, five, and ever upward.

Boundary setting is also a crucial practice which will help you not *feel inferior*. Personal boundaries are developed by our *thoughts* about the reasonable, safe, and permissible ways that people can treat us. Boundaries protect us. We need to establish boundaries because there are toxic people in the world. These are the people who want to use us, dump their negativity in our lap, and try to make themselves feel better by putting us down. Their behaviors can help us realize growth is an inside job. Change your thoughts to letting these toxic people go and protect yourself. You will no longer be a slave to their negativity. You will be the master of your destiny. You will not, as Eleanor Roosevelt said, give them *consent*, to *make you feel inferior.*

Charlie was raised in a house where personal boundaries were not taught or respected. Charlie was the youngest of five brothers whose dad was a sales rep and was gone most work days. Mom did her best to raise the boys but was overwhelmed and could not stop the physical and emotional fighting that occurred on a daily basis.

Charlie came to my office as a 27-year-old, gainfully employed professional, but unhappy in his personal relationships. During our first session, Charlie said he felt like the runt of the litter in his family of origin. He tried to be good, measure up, and keep up with his older brothers, but they made fun of him and picked on him. Charlie learned what was reflected to him: that he was not good enough and had to take the abuse.

Charlie dated women who were emotionally tough on him and expressed in a variety of ways that he never measured up. Charlie said that he tried to make his significant others happy, but the feedback he received was he never had enough money, never said the right things, and didn't do it enough to make them happy.

Charlie said that he had no self-esteem and wondered if he could ever be successful in a relationship. Our therapeutic work started by shining a light so that Charlie could see that he had learned many unhealthy—and untrue—things about himself in his family of origin. During our sessions, Charlie learned how to set boundaries and the criteria for a healthy relationship. Charlie discovered the traits he liked about himself.

In our last session, I shared the Eleanor Roosevelt quote with him. He smiled and wrote it down in his notebook. He looked up and said, "I will no longer give consent to anyone and allow them to make me feel inferior."

Truth #1: *Your thoughts create your reality.* Charlie's thoughts about himself were what he learned in his childhood. This created low self-esteem and unhealthy relationships. Charlie changed his thoughts about himself and created better self-esteem and mutually respectful relationships.

Truth #2: *There is no reality outside your interpretation of it.* Charlie interpreted his social relationships to mean that he was doing something wrong. After he learned why he interpreted life that way, he changed his thoughts about himself and gained a new view of the same social reality.

Truth #3: *You are not your thoughts.* Charlie learned to see his thoughts. He realized that when the old thoughts of "You are not measuring up," bubbled up in his mind, he could let that go and created healthier thoughts.

The only people who get upset when you boundaries are the ones benefitting from your having none. Speak your truth. Say "no" when something doesn't feel good. Gandhi said, "I will never let anyone walk through my mind with their dirty feet." Allow no one to make you feel inferior. Only you can stop them from making your mind a dirty pig pen. Author and inspirational speaker Brene Brown said, "Daring to set boundaries is about having the courage to love ourselves when we risk disappointing others." Love yourself. You're worth it!

Reflections

1. Name an area in your life where you are complaining about how another person treats you. Realize growth is always an inside job. What do you need to do to create a better environment for yourself?
2. Where do you need to say "yes" to yourself, which might mean saying "no" to someone else?
3. Is there someone in your life who needs to hear more often about the positive traits you see in them? Practice giving more positive reinforcement than punishment or negative feedback. How does that make you feel?

Chapter 19

S

"There is nothing either good or bad, but thinking makes it so. "

William Shakespeare

Shakespeare was an English poet, playwright, and actor. His plays have been translated into every major language and are performed more often than any other playwright.

Hamlet Act 2, Scene 3:
Guildenstern: "Prison, my Lord?"
Hamlet: "Denmark's a prison."
Rosencrantz: "Then I guess the whole world is one."
Hamlet: "Yes, quite a large one, with many cells and dungeons. Denmark being one of the worst."
Rosencrantz: "We don't think so, my Lord."
Hamlet: "Well then, it isn't one to you, for there is nothing either good or bad, but thinking makes it so. To me it's a prison."

Shakespeare's quote has two of the core teachings. This first is this book's Truth #2: *There is no reality outside your interpretation of it.* Hamlet's interpretation of Denmark is it's a prison. He feels trapped and helpless to change his situation. Any control and freedom he thought he had dissipated with the murder of his father. Rosencrantz and Guildenstern are childhood friends of Hamlet who have had different life circumstances. Their interpretation of Denmark is positive and not marked by murder.

The second teaching uses the first half of Shakespeare's quote, *"There is nothing either good or bad."* As children we were taught the opposite of this. Obviously, we need to teach our children how to live successfully in the world. Better and more liberating language in which to make decisions is to ask, is this choice functional or dysfunctional, productive or non- productive, healthy or unhealthy? These are better words to use because we don't completely understand what is "good" or "bad."

There is a story from China that proves this point well. There was an old farmer who had only one horse and one son to help him on his farm. One day the horse escaped and all the farmer's neighbors felt sad for him. They told him they were sorry for his bad luck. The wise farmer said, "Good luck? Bad luck? Who knows? We shall see." A couple of days later, the horse came back with five wild mares. This time the neighbors congratulated the farmer on his good luck. His wise reply was, "Good luck? Bad luck? Who knows? We shall see." A week later, his son was taming one of the wild horses and got bucked off and broke his leg. Again, the neighbors expressed their sadness, and thought this was very bad luck. The farmer responded the same way, "Good luck? Bad luck? Who knows? We shall see." Some weeks later, the army came through his small village and rounded up all the young men to go off to war. When they found the farmer's son with a broken leg, they left him behind.

Do you feel the freedom and openness in the farmer? By accepting and not attaching to the "good" and "bad" he doesn't get blown around by the winds of external circumstances. He lives more in a state of equanimity, which arises from the power of observation—the ability to see without being caught by what we see. This practice creates peace, patience, and love. Labeling life as "good" and "bad" creates mental and spiritual ruts. This has also caused us to have a very short-sighted, egotistical view of most of our life circumstances. This thinking has stymied us to the point we rarely see the big picture.

I shared in Chapter 8 the question that Einstein thought everyone should answer: Do you believe the Universe is friendly, hostile, or a combination of the two? I believe the Universe is friendly. My practice is to avoid labeling the external circumstances in my life as "good" or "bad," because I really don't know. Sometimes I give myself a grade of "C" with this practice. There are times when anger and impatience are at the edge of my consciousness. An "F" is when I react with anger and use harsh words. When my practice is more at the "A" level, I am flexible and adaptable to find the lesson, move from unproductive to productive thoughts, and create healthier outcomes. I am also more compassionate toward myself, others, and all of life. I am grateful for the lesson and trust in whatever may come next.

The contemporary Christian song, *Blessings,* by Laura Story, is a beautiful song which speaks to this truth. Story's intriguing lyrics:
        "cause what if your blessings come through raindrops
        What if your healing comes through tears
        What if a thousand sleepless nights are what it takes to know You're near
        What if trials of this life are Your mercies in disguise?"

The practice of trusting life and not seeing everything as "good" and "bad' is not simple. We have a deeply ingrained habit of labeling life this dichotomous way. The first step is to understand the truth of the old

Chinese story of the farmer and the lyrics of *Blessing.* The second step is to use the new language of functional or dysfunctional, healthy or unhealthy. The third step is to name your lesson and take steps to live a more productive life. Lastly, lean into trusting Life more, and in time, see the benefits from all of your life circumstance.

Since Mother Earth is a big, old schoolhouse, everything in life is a lesson. Everything that happens is offered as a gift or a healing. We can make unhealthy, non-productive decisions, and stay stuck in our lesson plan. Or we can make functional, productive decisions, and spiral up to a healthier level of existence.

Most people come into my counseling office because something "bad" has happened in their life. At some point in the counseling process, I share the Chinese parable about the farmer. I challenge the client to see if they can create "good" out of the "bad."

Shelby came into my office dejected because another guy was "using her." She was tired of her current boyfriend who couldn't pay his part of the rent and utilities because of being underemployed or unemployed. She said that she had tried to help him—and other boyfriends—to live up to their potential.

Through the counseling process, Shelby learned that she was *thinking* in a co-dependent way. She saw in herself the classic symptom that she had to fix others and couldn't be happy unless others were happy. She began to accept responsibility and see that living this way was unhealthy and non-productive. Shelby reached the point of being thankful for the "bad" behaviors of her boyfriend because she could use the situation to learn her lessons and create "good" in her own life. Shelby learned her life lesson and slowly, incrementally, learned how to *think* and then live a different way and find healthier relationships.

Truth #1: *Your thoughts create your reality.* Shelby thought it was her job to save others. These thoughts created the reality of finding men who needed fixing. The men had thoughts that allowed them to live below their potential. They found women who were responsible and would pay the rent for them. These two non-productive ways of thinking created an unhealthy hamster wheel.

Truth #2: *There is no reality outside your interpretation of it.* Most of us create bi-polar realities of "good" and "bad." This allows the external events in our lives to determine our happiness. Changing to an internal sense of control, not interpreting these events as good or bad, and looking for our lessons and trusting Life will create more happiness and contentment.

Truth #3: *You are not your thoughts.* Shelby's true self is not co-dependent. Her thinking made her co-dependent. You are not any negative label you have given yourself. Your thinking has created unhealthy outcomes in your life. You can change your thinking to create healthier outcomes.

"To thine own self be true," is another famous line from *Hamlet.* Your true nature is a fully functioning and loving person. We lose this because we have accepted the "bad" that others have reflected to us, and the "bad" labeling we put on ourselves. Change your way of thinking and let go of "good" and "bad." Adopt the categories productive and non-productive, healthy and unhealthy. Learn your life lessons and merge into your true self.

Reflections
1. Name something that you have labeled "bad" in your life. Step back and humorously say to yourself,

"The horse ran away." With this mental space, discern now what is the healthiest response.
2. Is there someone in your life who is interpreting a similar life circumstance in a healthier way than you? Interview that person and ask why he/she has that viewpoint. Notice how your ego mind doesn't want you to let go of your unhealthier thoughts. Smile, change your thoughts, and lean into Shakespeare's idea that "thinking will make it so."
3. Journal on Laura Story's lyric, "What if trials in this life are Your mercies in disguise?" How can you make one of your "trials a mercy in disguise?"

Chapter 20

T

"My legacy is that I stayed on course from beginning to end, because I believed in something inside of me."

Tina Turner

Tina Turner is a singer, songwriter, and actress. She is one of the best-selling artists of all time, has sold more than 200 million records, and has won 12 Grammy Awards. In her autobiography, she revealed that she experienced severe domestic abuse by her husband Ike Turner. After her divorce she launched a major comeback and built her own career.

There are many teachings that direct us to first look inward—at ourselves—for personal growth and happiness. "The journey forward is the journey inward." "Happiness is an inside job." "The kingdom of God resides within." "You will be exactly as happy as you decide to be." "When you point one finger, there are three fingers pointing back at you." "Don't focus on the speck in your brother's eye while ignoring the log in your own." "The only person I can change is myself." "Change yourself and you will change your world."

When aspects of our lives are not working out, why is our first reaction usually to blame the external circumstances and not look at our self? The answer is our ego mind—our dark side—which is never interested in personal growth and well being. It is easier to blame than to take responsibility. It is easier to find fault in others than to find it in yourself. It is easier to complain and stay stuck than to " ... stay the course from beginning to end because (you) believe in something inside of (you)."

Many people have tragic childhoods. Their parents are abusive, erratic, or absent. Many stay stuck in negativity and rarely find true happiness. Some transcend their harmful and damaging childhoods and become successful, happy adults. Research shows these resilient people had (1) another adult who entered their life in a positive manner, (2) a higher level of intellect, and (3) an internal sense of control and understood their thoughts create their reality.

I firmly believe that circumstances don't have to dictate one's destiny. I wouldn't be a psychotherapist if I didn't whole-heartedly believe this. I share the research on resilient people with clients to help them transcend their difficult childhoods. The recipe for growth and healing is to first look toward yourself.

American author David Foster Wallace said in a 2005 commencement speech at Kenyon College, " ... the choice of what to think about is our greatest power." We can think about external circumstances or we can think about what we think about external circumstances. The choice is ours. We do not have much power over external circumstances. We have 100 percent power over the thoughts we decide to identify with and act upon.

For example, you are having difficulty finding a job that is a good fit for you. You can blame the economy, or all the different Human Resource Departments. Or, you can look at your own thoughts. Have you thought about how well-prepared you are and are you going into the interviews with the best resume? Have you thought about being on the cutting edge in a profession or occupation and are you aware of the latest technology in this area of expertise? Do you believe that you are the absolute right person for that position?

Believe in something inside of you that will exude the best energy to be the right fit for that job. *Believe in something inside* of you that has the persistence to keep knocking on doors. *Believe in something inside* of you that has the tenacity to learn cutting edge research so you will bring that something extra to the table.

Thomas had been in and out of counseling with me for years. He had a drug and alcohol addiction problem that he never truly owned. When he would get into trouble at home or work, he would talk around the specific issue, but never talk about the core issue of addiction.

Thomas had charm and charisma. This was a blessing and curse. It was a blessing because people liked him. He could quickly create friendships and win people over. It was a curse because people liked him, would forgive him for his alcohol-induced problems, and life would continue as before.

This time, Thomas came in for counseling when his wife was at the end of her rope and had kicked him out of the house. Thomas had tried everything he had done before to win his wife back. He quit drinking, bought her flowers, and turned on his charm.

"Why has she not let you back in the house this time, Thomas?" I asked him.

"I picked up our daughter from school, and I was a little drunk." He looked down. "It was stupid, I know."

I paused. I didn't see that one coming. He continued talking. "I think I hit bottom. I need to either go to treatment, or attend AA meetings."

"Maybe both," I offered.

"Yeah, and I'm not looking forward to it." He paused. "This isn't going to be easy."

"I have suggested treatment before. Why are you considering it this time?"

"Because my wife isn't budging."

"Why is that making you change?" I asked, to help him own his path to recovery.

"I don't want to lose my family. Since she isn't changing and letting me back in, I need to change."

"Do you want to call a treatment center from my office?"

He hesitated and smiled. "Yeah, no time like the present."

Thomas was starting a new course where he would find the strength inside of him to maintain his sobriety.

Truth #1: *Your thoughts create your reality.* For years, Thomas had thoughts that turning on his charm and charisma would make people forgive him. This allowed Thomas to stay a drunk. Thomas changed his thoughts when his wife wouldn't forgive him. These thoughts created a reality of a 30-day treatment program.

Truth #2: *There is no reality outside your interpretation of it.* The people in Thomas's life interpreted his promises of quitting drinking as real. It took the severe situation—of Thomas driving his daughter while under the influence—for his wife to change her interpretation of his drinking. A new reality was created where she set strong boundaries and didn't allow him to live in their house.

Truth #3: *You are not your thoughts.* Thomas used to think; *My wife will forgive me if I quit drinking for a while, promise the world to her, and turn on the charm.* These thoughts led Thomas to never own his addiction. Now Thomas is thinking; *I need to stop drinking and go to treatment because I'm not allowed to move back home.* Thomas is neither of these thoughts, but these thoughts will lead Thomas down two different paths.

Lao Tzu, a 4th century BC Chinese philosopher and founder of Taoism said, "He who conquers others is strong; He who conquers himself is mighty." Tina Turner was mighty and "stayed the course from beginning to end because (she) believed in something inside of (her)."

Thomas was claiming his might by admitting that he had an addiction problem and then doing the necessary work not to have it run and ruin his life. One of the secrets to being mighty is to look at yourself first, be aware of your thinking process, and change your thoughts to those that will get you on the road to recovery and freedom.

Reflections

1. Tina Turner said, "I believed in something inside of me." Make a list of your traits—which are inside of you—that will help you more fully stay your course "from beginning to end."

2. Name an area of your life where you are blaming an external circumstance. Turn the camera to yourself and your thoughts. How can you take ownership and change your thoughts, which will change your world?

3. What legacy do you want to leave behind? Volunteering and making a difference? Loving your family? Creating something new? Something in your professional life? Everything starts with a thought. Start creating that legacy.

Chapter 21

U

"Wars begin in the minds of men, and in those minds, love and compassion would have built the defenses of peace."

U Thant

U Thant was a Burmese diplomat and the Secretary-General of the United Nations from 1961-1971. He was the first non-European to hold this position. His elevation to the highest executive position in this international organization was one of the key indicators of the new importance of the Asian nations.

U Thant is referring to wars against other sovereign nations. Most of us will never be in a position to declare war and send troops overseas or to a neighboring country. We can declare "war" on people who look different than us, people we do not understand, family members, and against our selves when we are overly critical.

"I want what you have." "I don't like you because you worship a different God." "I feel uncomfortable because you have a different sexual orientation." "I am better than you because of my skin color." "I hate myself because I screwed up again." "I would be better off dead because no one likes me."

All of these statements are merely thoughts. They have immense power behind them because the pronoun "I" starts each thought. (As we saw with the positive "I" statements discussed in earlier chapters.) Pronouns help indicate a person's focus of attention. When a person feels more insecure, self-conscious, or devalued, he is more likely to focus his thoughts and feelings on himself. A person who tends to use the pronoun "we" is more likely to consider the thoughts and feelings of others. She is open to working together to support, lift up, and invest in others.

The pronoun "I" can be fueled by ego thoughts. Thoughts from the ego mind are, by definition, only interested in self and will manipulate, control, and even declare war to get what it wants.

Thoughts of peace are found in the willingness to get outside oneself and listen to another person. Peace has the goal of overcoming differences, not forcing one's will onto another. Thoughts of peace include tolerance and respect. Thoughts of war include closed mindedness and impatience in one's desires.

The Buddhist concept of karma states that one's actions and thoughts lead directly to future consequences. The Christian scripture of what you sow, so shall ye reap is saying the same thing. So, if you sow thoughts of derision and hostility, you will reap that. If you sow thoughts of tolerance, love, and respect, you will reap that.

Many people have been raised and conditioned to think only about themselves. This leads to road rage, bitterness, estrangements, and unresolved conflicts. Every person can overcome their conditioning and claim a higher purpose. Start being aware of your knee-jerk thoughts; your reactive thoughts. Change them to thoughts that are more in line with your true purpose of loving your neighbor and creating peaceful inner and outer experiences.

My point is illustrated in a story that gives a picture of what heaven and hell are like. In hell, everyone is at a banquet table with wonderful, delicious food in front of them. Their forks and spoons are very long—so long that they can't turn them to their mouth and feed themselves. So the people in hell have pleasurable food in front of them, but they are starved throughout eternity.

In heaven, the people are also sitting at a banquet table with delicious food. Their forks and spoons are also so long that they can't feed themselves. But the folks in heaven use their eating utensils to feed the people across from them. They actually give the food to each other. This way, everyone is nourished and has a heavenly experience. Thinking only of yourself leads to wars and hell on earth. Thinking of *both* yourself *and* others to create win-win outcomes are the "defenses of peace," and heaven on earth.

Jason was 16-years-old and suspended from school for verbally assaulting a peer. His single mom took off work early to bring him to my office. Jason sulked in his chair while his mom gave me a family history. "I feel terrible," the mom started, "because I stayed with Jason's dad too long. He was verbally abusive to me and Jason. When he drank, he became mean and said terrible things to us."

I looked at Jason while his mom dabbed her eyes with a Kleenex. "I'm sorry Jason."

"You didn't do anything," he responded.

"I know I didn't, but I feel bad that your dad was abusive to you and your mom."

"He's a dick."

"And, he's missing out on a great kid."

Jason looked at me like I was crazy. "Jason, you've exhibited some unhealthy behaviors that have brought you into my office. But your mom told me on the phone you're kind to your little sister, and you volunteer at the Capital Humane Society because you want to be a vet." Jason's mom grabbed another Kleenex and Jason sat up a little straighter in his chair. "Jason, you have hurt and anger inside of you because of how your dad treated you. You thought you could get rid of it by bullying the other kid in school. Did that get rid of the hurt and anger?"

"No," he replied.

"Then I hope you and I can spend some time together, so you can release that negative old stuff and you can be who you really are---a kind, compassionate, and smart kid."

Jason and I met for many weeks. Wars did begin in his mind because he was emotionally wounded from his dad's verbal abuse. We spent time healing those wounds, building a stronger, healthier sense of self, so in that same mind, love and compassion were built. Jason's conditioning, which caused him to see the world as hostile, was changed. He was aware when those thoughts would resurface. He would change his thoughts and see his peers' behaviors as juvenile, set boundaries, and move away from a potential fight.

Truth #1: *Your thoughts create your reality.* Jason had thoughts that other people's remarks were disrespectful and he had to fight fire with fire. Jason changed his thoughts to seeing other people's words as immature and would walk away from the situations. His first set of thoughts created a reality of school suspension. The second set of thoughts "built the defense of peace."

Truth #2: *There is no reality outside your interpretation of it.* Jason created a reality of getting himself into trouble by interpreting his peers' behaviors as confrontational. Jason created a healthier reality by interpreting those same behaviors as juvenile.

Truth #3: *You are not your thoughts.* It is normal for children to accept the words their parents say to them. In Jason's case, he had the thoughts that he was a bad kid because that is what his dad told him. Jason bullied others because he had been bullied by his dad. When Jason realized those words from his dad were not true, he changed his perception of himself, which changed how he acted in school.

Michael Jordan, one of the all-time greatest professional basketball players said, "My mother is my root, my foundation. She planted the seed that I base my life on, and that is the belief that the ability to achieve starts in your mind." What do you want to achieve? War and unresolved conflicts, or love, compassion, and peace? Both are manifestations from your mind. You can actually believe you can stop internal and external wars instead of merely keeping them at bay. Your thoughts create your reality. This is powerful. You are powerful.

Reflections

1. Catch yourself when you feel you're living your life too centered around "I." Change your thoughts and create a "we" outcome where both sides win.
2. You, like everyone, are conditioned to think and act in a certain way. Not all of it is healthy. Be open when you are receiving negative feedback which is showing you your unhealthy conditioning. Now, create new thoughts that create better outcomes.
3. " ... the ability to achieve starts in your mind." Start creating a legacy of "love and compassion."

Chapter 22

V

"A film can open hearts and minds that have been closed, for whatever reason."

Vanessa Redgrave

Vanessa Redgrave is an English actress of stage, screen and television. Redgrave received the 2010 British Academy of Film and Television Arts Fellowship. She is a political activist and was elected to serve as a UNICEF Goodwill ambassador.

        M. Scott Peck's famous first sentence of *The Road Less Traveled* is "Life is difficult." One of Buddha's interpretations of this same point is, "Life includes suffering." I think everyone would agree with these statements. For example, family members die. Friends move on. Husbands and wives divorce. Boyfriends and girlfriends break up. A close friend can't get a grip on his addiction. We lose our job at no fault of our own.
        Buddha also said pain is inevitable, suffering is optional. All these examples are painful. A break up, losing a job, or the death of a family member makes us feel vulnerable. A mental habit is to close our heart because we think that will save us from further pain. The opposite is true. By closing our heart, we are creating the suffering that Buddha said is optional.
When we create the thoughts that close our heart, we are no longer available to feel happiness, joy, love, or have any fun.

Our ego mind does not like it when things happen that are outside of our control. When we think we are creating a good defense against life—by shutting our heart—we are actually perpetuating the suffering.

We cannot stop our workplace from being bought by a larger corporation and then being part of the downsizing process. We cannot control an alcoholic. We cannot control whether someone breaks up with us. We do have the power to shift our thinking about these external circumstances, open our heart again, and then prayerfully invite the next best job, the next best life partner, or go to Al-Anon and learn not to be pulled into the alcoholic's tornados.

You read about paradoxes in Chapter 17. One of my favorite paradoxes is "Having an open heart is the safest place to be." If your heart is open, you are safe because you will forgive and continue to love the person who is acting inappropriately. You will not take things personally. If you have an open heart, you will trust your Higher Power and honor the grief process. If you have an open heart, you will not continue to suffer because you are in a state of love.

I want you to have a strong backbone and set boundaries while you are keeping your heart open. I don't want anyone to take advantage of you or walk over you. Combining strength of character and compassion is like being a peaceful warrior in the world full people with many different motivations.

Buddha taught there are four divine abodes: compassion, loving-kindness, equanimity, and taking joy in the joy of others. Buddha said that these qualities are always available to us if we choose to live with an open heart. These states of being are much better than resentment, anger, and loneliness.

We have examined the closed-heart and open-heart dynamics. Now, I would like you to examine if you are open-minded or closed-minded? The vast majority of people would answer they are open-minded. That is like Garrison Keillor's Lake Wobegon where " ... all the children are above average."

We are all somewhere on the spectrum of open to closed-minded. Closed-minded people are more interested in being "right" than in getting the healthiest, most productive outcomes. Closed-minded people tend to have smaller worlds because they are not open to ideas and people who are different. Closed-minded people are more prone to anxiety, depression, and anger because they are not open to when something unexpected happens.

Warren Buffet of Berkshire Hathaway is one of the most successful investors of all time. Charlie Munger, the Vice Chairman of Berkshire Hathaway, is not as well known, but his insights on business and life are unique and correct with uncanny consistency. He said, "The human mind is a lot like the human egg, and the human egg has a shut-off device. When one sperm gets in, it shuts down so the next one can't get in."

Realizing you can also be closed-minded is the first step to not allowing the "shut-off device" to operate. Be open. Be curious. Ask questions. Try to see things through the other person's perspective. Be humble. The result of these practices will be a more complete understanding and better outcomes. It will also result in more happiness and less stress because you are open and adaptable to the situation at hand.

Redgrave's quote reminds us that a film, a piece of art, or a song can help open our heart and mind again. Seeing a love story on the big screen can create a thought that will tug us toward being open to a new relationship. Hearing a moving song can create a thought to open our mind and heart and forgive someone. Seeing a painting can evoke feelings of wanting to feel joy again.

Louise came into counseling four years after her husband told her he wanted a divorce and moved out that day. Louise was left with two young boys ages 10 and 8.

Her children were now 14 and 12, well adjusted, doing well in school, with many friends. Louise was not hurting financially, had a good group of friends, but she was still angry. She knew she should move on with her life, but she didn't know how to.

I asked Louise, "Do you have a closed heart?" Tears immediately welled in her eyes. "I don't with my children, but I know I do everywhere else in my life." Louise had much to get off her chest so she told about how she had been devastated by her husband leaving her. Louise let me know that her ex was a salesman, life of the party, and had never really grown up. She had to take care of all the home finances and raise the children.

The next session I asked Louise what she feared about opening her heart again. She gave me a surprised look. "I think it's pretty obvious. I don't want to be hurt that bad again."

"I don't want you hurt that bad again either. You are smarter now. I think you have learned your lesson and will not date a life-of-the-party-guy who is still emotionally an adolescent. I think you're ready to open your heart and date again."

She leaned her back and head against the sofa, as if to allow my statement to pass right by her. Tears welled again.

"My friends have guys they want to line me up with."

"Louise, you told me you want to let go of the anger. The anger is still in your heart because its trapped in your closed heart. I think you are ready to take some calculated risks and incrementally open your heart."

She smiled. "Maybe I am. Maybe I am."

Truth #1: *Your thoughts create your reality.* Louise had thoughts of never allowing herself to be vulnerable with a man again. She created a reality of anger. When Louise changed her thoughts and opened her mind and heart again to enter the dating world, her reality was less angry and more filled with fun and excitement.

Truth #2: *There is no reality outside your interpretation of it.* Louise interpreted her husband leaving her as catastrophic and promised herself that she would never allow herself to be in a relationship again where she could be hurt so badly. Louise changed her interpretation to the seeing the need to learn her lesson and not date a similar kind of man. This allowed her to change her reality to one of dating other kinds of men.

Truth #3: *You are not your thoughts.* Louise had non-productive thoughts that created a closed mind and closed heart. Deep down, she knew that was not her true self, but she didn't know how to escape that hell. Since she was not those thoughts, she changed the thoughts that allowed her to create some heavenly experiences.

Helen Keller said, "The most beautiful things in the world cannot be seen or even touched, they must be felt with the heart." This is your life—allow yourself to experiencing the "beautiful things" by opening your heart. Napoleon Hill (Chapter 14) said, "A closed mind stumbles over the blessings in life without recognizing them." This is your life—allow yourself to see the blessings that are all around you by opening your mind.

Reflections

1. You are on the continuum of open-minded to closed-minded. Figure out where in your life you are more closed-minded. Ask a friend where he/she thinks you are closed- minded. Now, practice being open-minded on that subject. Read about it. Talk to someone about it. Write about it.
2. You are on the continuum of open-hearted to closed-hearted. Figure out where in your life you have a closed heart. Ask a friend where he/she thinks you have a closed heart. Remember, having an open heart is the safest place to be. Practice being open-hearted in that area of your life. Write about that experience. Share with a friend.
3. Watch a provocative movie. See how it opens your heart and mind. Take that insight and now live it in the movie you are creating in front of you which you call your life.

Chapter 23

W

"You don't get what you hope for. You don't get what you wish for. You get what you believe."

Oprah Winfrey

Oprah Winfrey is a talk show host, actress, media executive, and philanthropist. The Oprah Winfrey show was the highest-rated television program of its kind. Oprah reinvented her show with a focus on self-improvement and spirituality.

Why do some people walk into a crowded party and know they will be accepted and people will like them? Because they *believe* people will like them. Why do others walk into the same room, fearful and hesitant, knowing people are scary and might emotionally hurt them? Because they have this *belief* system.

Why do some athletes, who have the same skill level as others, win more often than not? Because they *believe* they are competitive and *believe* they will find a way to win. Oprah's quote is a lot like Kierkegaard's quote in Chapter 11 (Our life always expressed the result of our dominant thoughts). "What you believe" are your "dominant thoughts." That is why it is essential, vital and fundamental to your personal growth to spend time, excavate, and bring to the light your belief systems.

Debbie was the eldest girl of six children. Her parents were first generation wealthy and they enjoyed rubbing shoulders with the other wealthy people at a country club, dance clubs, and dinner parties. It was expected of Debbie to take care of the three younger children. Initially, Debbie was okay with this because she was a natural caregiver. But when Debbie reached adolescence, she wanted more freedom, but her parents did not allow that because of their social calendar. Debbie was conditioned to *believe* that she did not matter and it was her responsibility to make sure everyone else was okay.

Debbie married a handsome but depressed man. Because of her belief system, she thought she needed to take care of him and her wants and needs did not matter. The marriage lasted 20 exhausting years, but she left it when her son was successfully in his third year of college.

She came into my office depressed and anxious. "Why do I get walked over at work? I would never treat people the way they treat me! Why did I marry someone who was depressed? He was not interested in my welfare when we were dating *and* when we were married."

Debbie had already shared her family history with me. I asked her, "Do you see how you were conditioned as a child to *believe* you had to take care of others at your own expense? Do you see how that *belief* is repeated in your adult life?"

"Yes, but it's good to take care of others. I pride myself on that," she said a bit defensively.

"But not when it's at your expense," I responded.

My comment hit an emotional wound. Debbie reached for the Kleenex box. I continued. "Debbie, you tell me you want a better life partner, and a better boss. But if you believe that you don't deserve that, you will continue to find men who need to be taken care of, and a boss who does not care about you."

"How do I change that?" Debbie asked.

I shared this quote from Oprah with her. She was a big Oprah fan so she listened intently. I said the last line again. "You get what you believe." I paused. "What has been the belief that you've been getting?"

"I need to take care of everybody and I don't matter," she answered. Debbie dried her eyes with the same tissue.

"And, what do you want as a new belief?"

"I don't know. I'll have to think about it."

"Good idea. Interview some of your friends. Ask them what their beliefs are about their spouses and their bosses."

Many weeks later, Debbie was starting to integrate a new belief system where she wanted a supportive boss and a loving, supportive man in her life. Many weeks after that, a friend of hers—whom she had interviewed—told her there was a position opening where she worked. She loved her boss and the work. Debbie interviewed, gave her two-week notice, and secured a job where she "got what (she) believed."

A friend went to a workshop on the power of money. He shared with me a question that he found helpful. What is your first memory of money? A memory instantly came to me. I remembered as a 4th grader doing odd jobs around the house to earn money. My dad was a big proponent of saving 10 percent of what you earned. He bought my brother and me a glass bank with four slots. A slot for quarters, dimes, nickels, and pennies. We had to figure out what was 10% of what we were paid, and put those coins in each slot. I watched the coins inch their way up each column and then I could spend it on something with my parents' approval.

I instantly made a connection between what I *believe* about money and how it was spilling over into other parts of my life. I have the belief I have to be very aware about the nickels and dimes. I became frugal and had the propensity to be a penny pincher. I had the belief that you never touch your savings account.

"You get what you believe." That belief got me a life of seeing money as scarce and I had to save it. That belief stopped the flow of money. Once I brought to light these non- productive beliefs, I have practiced changing the beliefs. I am integrating the beliefs that money is abundant, and we will always have enough.

Saving money is healthy. I interpreted the event a certain, unhealthy way. My brother also had to save 10 percent, and he slid his coins down his glass bank. He interpreted it differently and did not have my same issue with money.

Buddhist monk and scientist Matthieu Ricard said, "We all want to be happy. There's a big difference between aspiration and achievement." I believe one of the main roads to happiness is the achievement of the discovery of your beliefs, letting go of the unhealthy ones we were conditioned to believe in as children, and develop healthier beliefs.

Truth #1: *Your thoughts create your reality.* Debbie's thoughts were conditioned by her parents in her childhood. She believed it was her job to take care of others. She also believed that her needs did not matter. She lived that for 50 years. Debbie did not know why she was so unhappy so she sought counseling. Debbie learned that she could adopt a new, healthier belief system. Soon afterwards, her life—her reality—was changing and Debbie was finding true happiness for the first time in her life.

Truth #2: *There is no reality outside your interpretation of it.* Debbie was in an unfulfilling marriage because her husband had never sought treatment for his depression. For many years, her interpretation of the marriage was she needed to work harder to "parent" and take care of her husband. Once she realized he was never going to change, she changed her interpretation of the marriage, saw that it was dysfunctional, and soon created a way to leave it.

Truth #3: *You are not your thoughts.* Debbie was not the thoughts her parents conditioned her to believe. Those thoughts guided her during her childhood and most of her adulthood. They were merely thoughts that had lots of power. Debbie changed those thoughts which then drastically changed her reality.

Oprah said on one of her shows, "The question is, What do you believe? Do you believe that you are worthy of happiness? Do you believe happiness, success, abundance, comfort, fulfillment, peace, joy, love is a part of your birthright? Is that what you believe or do you believe something else? Because you will manifest the life that you believe."

Reflections

1. Look at your life. You are manifesting your beliefs. Which area is not as healthy as you would like it to be? Change your belief about that area. Repeat as necessary.
2. What is your belief system about money? Do you believe money is scarce? Abundant? Spend some time looking at that belief because you will manifest what you believe.
3. Every parent conditions their children into beliefs. What are some belief systems your parents modeled and taught that you have decided are not productive for you? Write down new belief systems and "parent" yourself in a new, healthier way.

Chapter 24

X

"If the ox could think, it would attribute oxality to God."

Xenocrates

Xenocrates was a Greek philosopher, mathematician, and leader of the Platonic Academy
from 339 to 314 BC.

Talking about God can be as refreshing as a walk in the mountains next to a stream, or it can be as unbearable as seeing a tornado ripping apart your home. Most of us have been conditioned since our early childhood to have a certain belief system—thoughts—about God. This belief is usually intertwined with a structured religion and a place of worship: church, synagogue, or mosque.

Billy Sunday was the most influential American evangelist during the first two decades of the 20th century. He said, "Going to church doesn't make you a Christian any more than going to a garage makes you an automobile." Sadly, many people who profess to be a Christian live a life that doesn't even come close to the teachings of Jesus. Sadly, some people's God is one of punishment and retribution. They then treat loved ones with abuse and frame it as God's will. This has created a negative belief system about God with countless people.

Religion can be a place where abuse occurs, or it can be a place where life-sustaining spirituality occurs. Research shows that incorporating spirituality in our lives—believing in a loving God or Higher Being—can help us heal and transcend many earthly issues. Being aware of our thoughts, observing them and changing them can be helped by having a spiritual practice or outlook. That doesn't necessarily mean going to church or joining a religion. This can mean finding a place in nature, spending time with trusted friends, or in solitude where you learn how to incorporate love, tolerance, forgiveness, justice, and other values that help you and humankind heal and evolve.

When I include spirituality in this book, it is from many different faiths and teachers. No religion has the monopoly on truth. You have read truths from Jesus, Buddha, Gandhi, Native American religion, and Einstein who incorporated spirituality and science. Or, we could all just follow this simple truth spoken by the Dalai Lama: "My religion is kindness."

How successful are you operating your kidney today? What kind of grade do you give yourself for helping your body pass waste as urine? How well have you helped filter your blood before sending it back to your heart? How well are you operating your respiratory system? Are you consciously breathing or is your body breathing itself? You and I are not consciously running our kidneys and respiratory systems. I believe in a Creator, or as George Lucas refers to in Star Wars, The Force. This is an omnipresent energy of unfathomable intelligence, creativity, and love (to name a few of the attributes). The Force has lovingly created our bodies with an intelligence that is beyond amazing. This Great Spirit has also created Mother Earth, and the Universe.

The problem with most of us is that we don't acknowledge the miracle of our bodies and our ego mind takes over. We forget there is Something Greater Than We Are that is loving and benevolent. It wants whatever is best for us. We forget, grab the reins of our life, and set out on our own. We fall short, and stay stuck in this limited way of thinking, and dig in ever harder. We are then perpetually tired, unhappy, and feel somewhat like a victim.

During my time on Mother Earth, I believe I have free will and can make my own decisions. The problem with this is when I think "Pete can do it," I usually fall short. If I think "Pete and God and do this," something mysterious occurs and healthier outcomes occur.

Xenocrates is telling us to get out of our ego mind, and realize our humanness is from God, so include God in your life. Every day, be thankful for your kidneys and respiratory system (and every other organ). An attitude of gratitude creates more things in which to be grateful. This is a road to happiness. Every day, catch yourself when self-centered, egotistical ways of thinking occur. Let go of those thoughts, quiet your mind, then see the more loving, creative, supportive thoughts in which to manifest in your world.

Our default mode is operating from the ego mind. Our world is in disarray and in a chaotic mess because of this. Is your world in disarray and sometimes a chaotic mess? This is the needed feedback to change, and live and think in a different way.

The Bible says the fruits of the spirit are "love, joy, peace, forbearance, kindness, goodness, faithfulness, gentleness, and self-control." (Galatians 5: 22-23) Do you want your thoughts to create these fruits, or do you want your mind to create an alarming amount of distress?

You're far enough in this book to realize your thoughts create your reality. Make a commitment to consciously practice staying connected to your Higher Power. Make a commitment to learn more about how to live a life connected to The Force. Make a commitment to live more Christ-like, be connected to your Buddha nature, or become one with the Native American concept of the Great Spirit. Research shows you will be happier and healthier. I have seen this proven over and over with my clients, friends, and myself.

Tim was raised in an emotionally and physically abusive home. His dad was an alcoholic and used Old Testament scripture to parent Tim and his siblings. We all deify our parents, make gods of them. We then associate the parenting style of our parents to the "parenting" style of God.

In Tim's case, he saw God as judgmental and wrathful. Tim also inherited the addiction gene. This combination made him an angry drunk. A divorce, DUI, and receiving a one-week suspension from his job led him to my office. Tim told me he had been sober for a month. He indicated that his sobriety was driven by an external source—his workplace—and he was white knuckling the process. He was going to AA because of an external source—the courts.

Tim thought his boss was a jerk, his ex-wife a name I will not repeat, and all police officers some other objectionable term. When he told me about his family of origin, he called his dad an ass and his mom a passive co-conspirator. Tim, like most children of alcoholics, could never rely on a parent to take care of his needs, so they grew up to be too self-reliant. Tim also projected his view of his father on all authority figures, which included God. He saw them all as asses and out to get him.

Bill W., the co-founder of Alcoholics Anonymous, said "It seems absolutely necessary for most of us to get over the idea that man is God." The Alcoholics Anonymous book states alcohol is "an illness which only a spiritual experience will conquer." The second step in the AA twelve- step program is, "We came to realize that a Power greater than ourselves could restore us to sanity."

Tim was conditioned at an early age to think he had to protect himself and take care of himself. That is why he was not relying on a Higher Being or the AA program, and was white knuckling his recovery process. I reflected to Tim that he learned early on that he had to be self-reliant. Thinking this way saved him as a child. Now he, like all of us, had to allow others and a spiritual belief to help him navigate life. I suggested to Tim that he start working the second step of AA. I told him that I was an authority figure who was trying to help him. Hopefully he would open himself up and try not to see me as an ass who was out to get him.

I also shared with him that another word for alcohol was "spirits." I said that maybe he was using the wrong kind of spirit to help him in the world. There is a healthier Spirit which could be his Higher Power.

Slowly, incrementally, two steps forward and one step back, Tim kept his job, was staying sober one day at a time, and was even dating someone who wasn't "out to get him."

Truth #1: *Your thoughts create your reality.* Tim's thoughts were conditioned to believe all authority figures were negative and out to get him. This created a reality of resistance, hostility, and drinking to excess. When Tim worked his AA program and counseling assignments, he changed his thoughts which created a healthier, happier environment for him.

Truth #2: *There is no reality outside your interpretation of it.* Tim interpreted the world as hostile. He drank to drown out the heaviness and negativity of that reality. Tim changed his reality to believe that everyone is doing the best they can. Tim knew that he had shortcomings, as did others.

Truth #3: *You are not your thoughts.* Underneath Tim's tough exterior was a good guy who wanted to do well in the world. His thoughts created the "tough guy" and his thoughts created the "good guy." He is neither of those thoughts. They are behaviors that come from thoughts.

Richard Rohr, a Franciscan friar, author, and spiritual teacher said, "The people who know God well—mystics, hermits, prayerful people, those who risk everything to find God— always meet a lover, not a dictator." Including God, Higher Power/ Great Spirit, The Force in your life can help you transcend your earthly problems and find a life more filled with love.

Reflections

1. You do not need to believe in a God to be a good person. Research shows that believing in a Higher Being and attending a place of worship increases happiness. What are your thoughts on God/Higher Being? Are you open to finding a place of worship that will match your values?
2. Do you want to be more conscious and monitor your thoughts to see if they are coming from your ego mind or spiritual mind? If so, for a period of time, mentally take note of whether your thoughts are self-centered and critical of others, or more loving and accepting of others.
3. Keep a journal of gratitude. Every day list at least three things for which you are grateful. Increase the list to five things. Increase the list to ten things a day.

Chapter 25

Y

"Truly wonderful, the mind of a child."

Yoda

Yoda is a fictional character in the movies Star Wars. He is one of the most powerful members of the Jedi Order. He is a legendary warrior and above all a teacher who loves to pass on his wisdom. Yoda's deep attunement to the Force—a mysterious energy field that binds all living things and gives the Jedi their powers—comes from exploring, studying and practicing.

Go to a playground and watch young children play. Their minds have not yet been conditioned to discriminate against people of different colors. They will interact with anyone who will play with them. They are happy, light-hearted, forgiving, and fearless.

Jesus said in Matthew 18:3, "Truly I tell you, unless you change and become like little children, you will never enter the kingdom of heaven." Adults' minds can be taken over by the ego. The ego mind is all about taking care of self and is full of fear and pride. That is the opposite of what Jesus taught. Jesus wants us to be humble, forgiving, and full of love. Children's minds are open, sincere, and uncomplicated. Adult's minds can be closed, insincere, and very complicated.

Shunryu Suzcki wrote *Zen Mind, Beginner's Mind.* The first sentence of his book states, "In the beginner's mind there are many possibilities, but in the expert's there are few." Beginner's mind is a Zen Buddhist term and one of its fundamental teachings. It refers to having an attitude of openness, eagerness, and lack of preconceptions when studying any subject matter.

When a child is learning something new, he or she is fearless, highly interested, full of wonder, in the present moment, and open to everything. This is the beginner's mind. Anytime you learn something new, you are in the beginner's mind. You are in the present moment, open and available to all information. You enter into learning with a clean slate and don't have preconceptions of how something should be.

In adulthood, what happens to this mindset—this attitude—that gives us freedom, agility, and happiness? Once something becomes familiar, the mind becomes a terrible master. It tries to take over, recalling memories, and creating expectations and fears which stop us or slow us down. Our mind becomes overwhelmed with these thoughts and we lose our concentration. Our mind drifts to the past or to the future which takes us out of the reality of the present moment. The pure innocence of the beginner's mind, where everything is exciting, fresh, and new, becomes mired in the heaviness of wondering what other people think, fears of being wrong, and falling short of expectations. Life becomes heavy and you experience more unhappiness.

Let's compare the ego mind to the beginner's mind. The ego mind says, "You've fallen down nine times. It won't work." The beginner's mind says, "Get up ten times." The ego mind says, "You should already have completed this." The beginner's mind (humorously) says, "I am not going to *should* all over myself." The ego mind says, "You messed up with this in the past, it won't work in the future." The beginner's mind says, "I have let go of the past and future. I am fully in the present moment and fully open to this experience." Children (beginner's mind) tend to let go of anger and judgments relatively quickly. Adults (ego mind) tend to remember what happened years ago and hold on to the anger, bitterness, and judgments.

Rachel was a retired school teacher who came to one of my book talks. She set up a counseling session because she said she was in a funk. She started the sessions by saying, "I have been retired for two years, and I have found since I don't have the daily structure of work, I am floundering." She paused for a moment. "Basically, I am in a rut."

Once she referred to being in a rut, I asked a question. "When is the last time you've done something new and outside your box?"

"I don't have a lot of money, so it's been a long time," she answered.

"Luckily, you don't need a lot of money." I explained the concept of beginner's mind. She immediately identified with it because she had taught elementary aged students. I challenged her to enter into an experience with the beginner's mind.

"I wouldn't know where to start," she replied.

"It's early October and the leaves on the trees are a variety of shades of orange, red, yellow, purple, and magenta. Go to a park and practice being in the present moment with nature. Pick up a leaf that has fallen and examine it. See the texture and the various colors. Stand under the tree and see how the light bounces off the leaves. Sit on a bench and listen to all the sounds around you. You will hear the wind through the trees, birds chirping, maybe a siren in the background. Listen until you hear a symphony. Then move to your sense of smell. What is the smell of autumn? When you mind starts to wander, gently bring it back to the present moment. Be conscious of how you're feeling during this and afterwards."

"Sounds like a good assignment. Maybe I'll write a poem afterwards."

A smile crossed my face. "I look forward to hearing about your experiences and maybe even reading your poem." Before I stood up to get my calendar, I said one more thing. "I would like to challenge you again. Go to a park which has a pond or lake. I want you to be like a young child, kick off your shoes, and walk along the edge and kick up some water."

Rachel matched my smile. "You give tough assignments."

Truth #1: *Your thoughts create your reality.* When Rachel taught school, her thoughts were about lessons plans, grading assignments, and classroom management. This reality gave her meaning and purpose. After she retired, she lost that external structure for her mind to think about. Her thoughts then went to television, cleaning house, and other activities that she found meaningless. When she practiced living from the beginner's mind, her reality was a deep connection to her God and the wonder of nature.

Truth #2: *There is no reality outside your interpretation of it.* Rachel's interpretation of retirement was depressing. Her interpretation was that she finally got to do nothing. She changed her interpretation of retirement to learning new skills and new ways of being in the world.

Truth #3: *You are not your thoughts.* Rachel was not her initial thoughts of retirement. These thoughts led her to feelings of malaise. Rachel was also not her thoughts of getting outside the box and living from the beginner's mind. These thoughts created a spiritual connection and writing poetry which she hadn't done since high school.

Yoda also said, "Do. Or do not. There is no try." It will take effort to change your habit of thinking like an adult, which includes staying with what you know and being averse to new ways of doing things. It will take effort to live out of "the mind of a child." It will take effort to "become like little children." Socrates said, "Wonder is the beginning of wisdom." Make a commitment to seeing things with wonder, openness, eagerness, and without fear. Beginner's mind is not a philosophy, it is a practice. If you choose to practice, the Force will be strong within you.

Reflections

1. Go to a park and play. Throw a Frisbee. Walk barefoot at the edge of a lake. Playfully kick some water on a friend.
2. When is the last time you sat in awe and felt humble? We adults rarely allow these experiences and feelings. Figure out what you will do to experience these feelings.
3. Do you feel the Force is strong in you? Practice living from the beginner's mind. It is "truly wonderful."

Chapter 26

Z

"The more aware of your intentions and your experiences you become, the more you will be able to connect the two, and the more you will be able to create the experiences of your life consciously. This is the development of mastery. It is the creation of authentic power."

*Gary **Z**ukav*

Gary Zukav is an American spiritual teacher, public speaker, and author of four New York Times bestselling books.

I have not written about the word intention yet. It is another very important facet of thinking. The dictionary defines intention as "a determination to act in a certain way." Where does the "determination" come from? You're reading the last chapter and you now understand ... your mind.

By being aware of your thoughts—your intentions—you have the power of choosing or determining every action you make. The key is to be aware of your intentions. Most of the adolescents who come into my office are not aware of their *intentions*. They definitely have not developed *mastery*.

I do a fun experiment in my office with them. First, we decide on the definition of the word intention. Then I ask the teen to share with me his/her top three intentions for the next two months. They say things like, "Go to school, get good grades, and stay out of trouble." I write them down and then go to my desk and pull out a small weight that is tied to an 8 inch string. I have them sit at my desk and hold the string with their dominant hand. I tell them to hold the string still and not move their hands or arms. I then say, "With your mind, I want you to visualize and move that weight left to right." I move my hand left to right so they know the direction. I say again, "With your mind move the weight back and forth." It starts moving ever so slightly. I compliment them and urge them to move it even further. It starts swinging left to right. I then say, "I want you to change your intention. Now move it from me to you." I move my hand that direction—which is 90 degrees different than the left to right. It takes a while, but the weight and string start moving that direction. I compliment them. Then I say, "Now, without moving your hand or arm, start moving the weight in a big circle." It starts to move immediately.

At this point the teens are smiling ear to ear. We stop and go back to our chairs. The teen is amazed. I start the conversation. "You just learned something most adults don't know. That is: whatever your intentions are, and you have control over them, they will come true." I pause to let that settle in. "I coached you to have intentions to move that weight. I coached you by words and hand movements to adopt those intentions. When the weight started moving, you started to believe in that intention yourself." I pause again. "Now, this isn't magic. You wanted to follow my instructions so your mind told your fingers to move their muscles ever so slightly. So slight, we couldn't really see them move. That created the initial movement. Your mind started to believe you could do it, so it continued to communicate to the muscles in your fingers. That's how you moved the weight."

I tell each adolescent that I have written their intentions in my notes, and in future weeks, we will truly see if these were really their intentions ... because they will come true! Usually they are proven wrong. They continue to skip classes, get poor grades, and continue to get into trouble. I read back to them their stated intentions and then tell them, "These are not your intentions. Your intentions is to have fun and say 'screw you' to all the rules."

They get defensive and say that the original list is truly their intentions. I say, "No they're not, because you have control over those things and they are not coming true. What's coming true is having fun and saying 'screw you.'" I then add, "I am not your parent or school administrator. My job as your counselor is to not give you consequences but make you aware of your intentions ... because they will come true."

Intentions are like dominant thoughts (Chapter 11) and beliefs (Chapter 23). We develop our intentions because we think they will us help navigate the world. We all attempt to predict and control the events in our lives. This is similar to that of the scientist who develops and tests hypotheses. Our intentions/beliefs/dominant thoughts serve as hypotheses that make the world meaningful to us. If these beliefs fit our life experiences, we find those beliefs to be useful and continue to use them in the future. If the beliefs and subsequent behaviors do not help us, we then change our beliefs and act accordingly.

Sadly, many people do not use this way of thinking. When life doesn't go according to their plans, they think from the ego mind and blame the environment—life conditions—and dig into their unhealthy and unproductive belief systems. What happens? Life expresses the result of their intentions and their lives incrementally become more unhappy and depressing. These are classic examples of the ego mind at work.

Typically, the intentions/dominant thoughts of people in the United States are (1) work hard in which to (2) make lots of money, so to (3) buy the latest fashions, bigger homes, sleeker cars, and newest gadgets. If "Our life always expresses the result of our dominant thoughts," what can life express in these people? Unhappy marriages. Detached relationships with children. Stress. Alcohol and drug abuse. Extramarital affairs. Heart attacks. Unhappiness.

Mythologist and author Joseph Campbell said, "There is perhaps nothing worse than reaching the top of the ladder and discovering that you're on the wrong wall." Palliative nurses often hear from the dying, especially from men, that they wished they hadn't worked so hard. They wished they had the courage to live a life true to themselves. They wished they had stayed in touch with their friends. They wished that they had allowed themselves to be happy. Their "ladders" were leaned against the wrong wall.

Many people don't test their hypotheses—their intentions—to see if they are guiding them to the life they want to live. Most people look around to see what everyone else is doing, assume that is correct, then fall in line.

Henry David Thoreau said, "Most men live lives of quiet desperation." Do you want to be like most people and have regrets on your death bed? No! Take some time now and be a scientist. Dust off your "microscope" and examine your thoughts. Write down which ones you think are dominant. Journal about them. Consider a new intention. How does that feel?

Truth #1: *Your thoughts create your reality.* If one of your intentions is "my net worth = my self-worth," then your reality will be one of working long hours, stressing about how your spouse spends money, and going into debt. If you change your intentions and exit the rat race, your reality might include a smaller house with a closer relationship with your spouse and children.

Truth #2: *There is no reality outside your interpretation of it.* A young adult is more likely to have the interpretation of working long hours, making lots of money, so to make a name of him or herself. A person who has lived that existence for many years starts to view a hectic work life as non-sustaining and looks for another job opportunity. He or she starts creating a new reality.

Truth #3: *You are not your thoughts.* The elderly man who is dying has different thoughts than when he was a young man. He realizes his thoughts of working long hours hurt many relationships. He wants to pass on his new insights to his adult son so he can create some distance between those powerful societal and familial-driven thoughts, let go of them so he doesn't repeat the lifestyle.

Reflections

1. Spend some time and be a scientist in which to discover your intentions. Do you like what you discovered? Do you feel like you have "developed mastery?"
2. Imagine you're on your death bed. Any regrets? Are you willing to take a risk and change a dominant thought/intention that led you to that regret?
3. Describe a lifestyle you would like to have. Fully describe the behaviors that are included in that lifestyle. Now write down the intentions that would create those behaviors and lifestyle. How does this feel? Communicate to a trusted person about this new thought—behavior—lifestyle.

Companion Guide (Cheat Sheet)

You learned in Chapter 1 that even though you might have learned in your childhood a certain unhealthy and dysfunctional way to think, you can now "entertain" those thoughts and not accept them. You can create new and *healthy* thoughts that will create a corresponding reality.

You learned in Chapter 2 that "you are what you think." If you think "bad thoughts," pain will follow. If you think "good" thoughts, *happiness* will follow.

You learned in Chapter 3 that if you think in a pessimistic way, you will "see difficulty is every opportunity." If you think in an optimistic way, you will "see *opportunity* in every difficulty."

You learned in Chapter 4 that your life conditions do not make you unhappy, it is how you view those conditions. *"Peace"* is the result of retraining your mind to process life as it is."

You learned in Chapter 5 that your thinking created certain problems. You cannot "solve the problem with the same thinking" you used that created the problem. If you change your thoughts about that life condition, your life could be more *productive.*

You learned in Chapter 6 that you have the *freedom* to choose your "attitude in any given set of circumstances." This is how your mind can be a wonderful servant.

You learned in Chapter 7 and 8 that your beliefs give you the ability to achieve your goals. Beliefs are the jet fuel that empowers *growth to* occur and helps you arrive at the life destination of your choice.

You learned in Chapter 9 that "bad cannot bother you unless you are available." Change your thoughts and then, instead of feeling bad, you will feel *good.* The Buddhist tradition teaches there are the Five Hindrances to living in a peaceful state. These hindrances are negative mental states that make us available to the "bad."

You learned in Chapter 10 that it is "done unto you" as you believe. If you believe the Universe if friendly, you will learn your life lessons and experience a sense of *harmony.* If a button of yours is being pushed, be grateful because that person or experience is showing up to shine the light on your button that needs to be healed.

You learned in Chapter 11 that "life always expresses the result of (your) dominant thoughts." If you can look at what you express in your life, you can work your way back and discover your dominant thoughts. Create more productive dominant thoughts and your life will be more *meaningful.*

You learned in Chapter 12 that your "knowledge" of everything is connected to your "perceptions." Everything is filtered through our perceptions. If we know we have a propensity to perceive a dynamic in our life as negative because of our childhood experiences, take time to incrementally change your perception to *abundance* and love.

You learned in Chapter 13 that you can "change your attitude" about something you don't like. If you don't change your attitude on a situation that you cannot change, you will suffer. That means the other person is not creating your suffering, you are. Take responsibility and change your attitude. The result will be a more *positive* life.

You learned in Chapter 14 that the thoughts you "conceive" in your mind, plus your "belief" that it's true for you, create the ability to "achieve" it in your life. This powerful formula will allow you to achieve things beyond measure and create a life of *purpose*.

You learned in Chapter 15 that your conscious and unconscious "I am" statements about yourself will always appear in your life. Knowing you created the mental and emotional state you are experiencing, allows you the power to create a new "I am" statement which will lead to more *beneficial* outcomes.

You learned in Chapter 16 that your mind has a habit of living in the "past and the future." When this occurs, your mind is a terrible master because it will create depressing thoughts and anxious states. Training your mind to be in the present moment will create contentment and even *bliss*.

You learned in Chapter 17 that embracing "both-and" paradoxical thinking leads to a bigger, more *fulfilling* life. You also learned that fear is the ego's way of destroying you. Find compassion for yourself and others because this is the best antidote to fear. Soon, you will "get an A" in the way you live your life.

You learned in Chapter 18 that "No one can make you feel inferior without your consent." Developing a healthy self-esteem is an inside job. When you find yourself thinking negatively about yourself, let go of those thoughts and create healthier thoughts. Boundary setting is also important when there are toxic people in your life who try and make you feel inferior. Surrounding yourself with healthy people and creating a healthy self-esteem leads to a life that is *grounded* and you can handle anything that appears in your life.

You learned in Chapter 19 that "There is nothing good or bad, but thinking makes it so." In our limited thinking, we can become stymied on our journeys because of something "bad" that has happened. If we change our thinking to perceive things as *functional* or dysfunctional, productive or non-productive, maybe we'll figure out how to create "good" out of the "bad."

You learned in Chapter 20 that believing "in something inside of (you)" can create a powerful life and "legacy." One of the best ways to create forward motion in life is to quit blaming your external circumstances, look within at your thinking process, and lean into your traits and qualities that can turn yourself around and solve problems/conflicts. *Self- determination* is a great strength.

You learned in Chapter 21 that "love and compassion have built the defenses of peace." Getting outside yourself, and de-powering what the pronoun "I" says that it wants, is the formula to create peace instead of war. If you sow thoughts of derision and hostility, you will reap that. If you sow thoughts of tolerance, love, and *respect*, you will reap that.

You learned in Chapter 22 that you "can open hearts and minds that have been closed." When you create the thoughts that close your heart, you are no longer available to feel happiness, joy, love, or have any fun. Practice having a strong backbone so you stand up against toxic behaviors. And, practice keeping your heart and mind open so you can grow, learn, and *evolve* into the person that is needed in the world.

You learned in Chapter 23 that "You get what you believe." You now know your thoughts create your reality. What you believe comes from your thoughts. If you believe you do not have much value, you will get a low paying job and non-fulfilling relationships. If you believe you have value, you will have a rewarding, good paying job and *gratifying* relationships. There is a direct correlation between your thoughts and your life.

You learned in Chapter 24 that our default mode is operating from the ego mind. We can also have a spiritual belief system and be connected to Something Greater Than Me. Including God, or as George Lukas calls it in *Star Wars*, The Force, can help us *transcend* our earthly problems and find a life more filled with love.

You learned in Chapter 25 that "the mind of a child" can create happiness, *light-heartedness*, and love. When a child learns something new, he or she is fearless, highly interested, and full of wonder. In adulthood, we lose this attitude and are not as open to change and possibilities. We need to reclaim the beginner's mind, and if we have fallen nine times, we need to get up ten.

You learned in Chapter 26 that "the more aware of your intentions ... the more you will be able to create the experiences of your life." Intentions are a determination to act in a certain way. Intentions are like dominant thoughts and beliefs. They serve as hypotheses that make the world meaningful to us. If these intentions fit our life experiences, we find those to be *useful* and continue to use them. If the intentions do not help us, hopefully we change our intentions and act accordingly.

Healthy. Happiness. Opportunity. Peace. Productive. Freedom. Growth. Good. Harmony. Meaning. Abundance. Positive. Purpose. Beneficial. Bliss. Fulfilling. Grounded. Functional. Self-determination. Respect. Evolve. Gratifying. Transcendence. Light-hearted. Useful. I don't know about you, but I want to live in the world these ways. How do I create these states? All twenty-six thought leaders say your thoughts create your reality. Be conscious, awake, and aware of your thoughts.

Everything starts with a thought.

Made in the USA
Columbia, SC
18 December 2020

28638632R00100